A Guide to Latin Meter and Verse Composition

David J. Califf

Anthem Press
London

First published by Anthem Press 2002
Anthem Press is an imprint of Wimbledan Publishing Campany,
PO Box 9779, London SW19 7QA

British Library Cataloguing in Publication Data
Data available

Library of Congress Cataloguing in Publication Data
A catalogue record has been applied for

ISBN 1 898855 72 2

1 3 5 7 9 10 8 6 4 2

Typeset by Mudra Typesetters - Pondicherry - India.
Printed by Bell & Bain Ltd., Glasgow

j. c. mckeown,

magistro,

et

discipulis academiae dominae nostrae

hoc opus gratissime inscriptum est

Cui dono illepidum, tiro rudis ipse, libellum?
en, Caprimulge, tibi: tu namque docere solebas
dempta rusticitate bonos me fingere uersus
et uobis, carae, sua sit pars muneris huius,
discipulae, quamquam uereor maiora canendo
ne argutos inter uidear strepere anser olores.

Contents

Contents

Preface

It has been nearly one hundred years since S. E. Winbolt asked, "Will the composition of Latin verse continue to form a part of our classical curriculum?"[1] The answer, it would seem, turned out to be, "No." Eton has not taught the subject for at least three generations, and today Oxford and Cambridge are lucky to have a half-dozen composition students between them in any given year. At a time when some graduate programs in classics are considering dropping their prose composition requirements, the making of Latin verses is scarcely taught to, much less required of, even those seeking a Ph.D. The question, then, that will inevitably greet a guide to Latin meter and verse composition is, "Why?"

One is tempted to respond with a paraphrase of Dante's remarks from *La vita nuova* on the difficulty of describing love to the loveless: It is impossible to explain the value of verse composition to anyone who is not already a faithful follower of the Muses, and to those who are, the rewards are obvious; consequently, there is no point in my clarifying any doubts because such clarification would either be useless or superfluous.[2] On the other hand, a few words in praise of verse composition would be no more out of place here today than they were in the prefaces of many nineteenth century textbooks.

If one is not persuaded by Charles Anthon's rather quaint claim that "original composition in Latin verse [is] an accomplishment which forms decidedly the truest and most enduring ornament of classical education,"[3] perhaps Richard Burnet's enumeration of its practical benefits will be more appealing.

I. It exercises, and of course strengthens, the memory.

II. It cultivates the taste.

III. It quickens the intellect, by the necessity of having recourse to perpetual contrivance to put together miscellaneous things regulated by certain laws.

IV. It strengthens the judgment, by the habit of selection.

V. It gives a more critical knowledge, not only of the Latin tongue, but of the force and nature of language in general, from the continual habit of considering the various and minutely-differing shades of meaning which distinguish words that would otherwise be taken for synonyms.[4]

---

[1] Latin Hexameter Verse (London: Methuen, 1903) vii.
[2] Cf. VN 14.56–73.
[3] Latin Versification (New York: Harper and Brothers, 1845) vii.
[4] Various English and Latin Poems (1808) 1–2.

Today's linguists have shown what Burnet already realized in 1808: that exercises in writing are as important to the process of language acquisition and development as practice in reading. Further, the current resurgence and success of oral Latin in both the schools and colleges confirms the instructional value of asking students to produce original sentences in Latin.

But just as Latin prose has its own particular rules of syntax, sentence structure, and style, and just as spoken Latin has its own conventions of expression, so too Latin verse functions according to a specific, if flexible, set of principles. The learning of these principles is facilitated by practice in composition no less than one's understanding of the rules of prose is reinforced by writing prose.

Putting it more strongly, J. C. McKeown once remarked that "if you can't write a hexameter, you can't read one." This may seem like an overstatement, but it is not, for the reading of poetry involves more than the comprehension of informational semantic content and more, too, than making sense out of a poem's figurative language and multiple layers of meaning. Poetry also consists of a complex array of verbal effects that are only ambiguously related to sense: its rhythms, sound patterns, and the arrangement of words within lines, couplets, or stanzas. While it is, of course, possible to recognize these effects in a poem without being able to write one, training in verse composition gives students a different and broader perspective on poetry and enables them to read it in a deeper, richer, and arguably more satisfying way. As Benjamin Franklin put it in a famous aphorism, "Tell me, and I forget. Teach me, and I remember. Involve me, and I learn."

If the composition of original Latin poetry is a prime example of "active learning," it is not merely a good academic exercise; it is also fun. At its best, verse composition can provide a welcome opportunity for creative expression, but even at a relatively unsophisticated level, it can be an enjoyable mental challenge, not unlike solving a puzzle. And like many good things, a Latin poem is even better when shared. Therefore, do not just write for school or for yourself but also for friends (and if they cannot read Latin, provide a translation). A gift becomes more generous, a thank-you note more charming, and congratulations more festive when accompanied by a Latin poem. Parting can be even sweeter sorrow in Latin verse, and the poem written for no particular reason is perhaps the nicest of all. Some people may think you are strange, but most will appreciate it, making your efforts all the more worthwhile.

PRELIMINARY REMARKS

The rules of Latin prosody and versification are so numerous and often seem so arcane and unforgiving that trying to commit them all to memory will surely sap all the joy out of reading and writing poetry. Some basic rules must be learned, of course, and a certain amount of technical analysis will deepen one's understanding and appreciation of the poet's art, but it can only be a beginning. Robert Pinsky, the former Poet Laureate of the United States, had it right when he wrote:

> Art proceeds according to the principles discernible in art. Therefore, if one is asked for a good book about traditional metrics, a good answer is: *The Collected Poems of William Butler Yeats*, or *The Complete Poems of Ben Johnson*. Two excellent books about so-called free verse are the two-volume *Collected Poems of William Carlos Williams* and *The Collected Poems of Wallace Stevens*. One of the most instructive books on short lines is *The Complete Poems of Emily Dickinson*. To learn a lot about the adaptation of ballad meter to modern poetry, an invaluable work is *Thomas Hardy: The Complete Poems*. No instruction manual can teach as much as careful attention to the sounds in even one great poem.[1]

The same principle applies to the study of Latin poetry. Some general guidelines are useful, but there is no substitute for individual observation and experience, and the exercises in this volume are designed not only to develop some fundamental skills but to engage the ancient poets directly. Accordingly, perhaps the most valuable exercise is one for which no textbook is needed: Read at least ten lines of Vergil, or Ovid, or Horace every day, and take a moment to think not just about the meaning of the words but their sound and rhythm as well. Firsthand familiarity with the ancient poets' actual practice will prove an invaluable resource for the modern student who wishes to write in their style.

---

[1] *The Sounds of Poetry: A Brief Guide* (New York: Farrar, Straus and Giroux, 1998) 7.

SECTION I: RHYTHM AND METER IN ENGLISH AND LATIN POETRY

Meter, broadly defined, is the patterned or "measured" (the word comes from μέτρον, measure) arrangement of recurring linguistic elements in poetry. Metrical patterns are potentially infinite in number but are often based upon such things as the number and sequence of syllables; patterns of accent, alliteration, or vowel sounds; or syntactic units such as the phrase, clause, or sentence.

Most modern English poetry (including free verse) is based upon patterns of *stress* or *accent*. In a Shakespeare sonnet, for instance, unaccented syllables alternate evenly with accented syllables:

My místress' eýes are nóthing líke the sún.

The rhythm used in this line—as in three quarters of all English poetry—is called iambic pentameter. Its smallest repeated metrical unit, or "foot," is the iamb (◡ –, an unaccented syllable followed by an accented syllable), and there are five (πέντε) iambs to a line. Words in English poetry should be stressed exactly as they would be in normal speech: Words of two or more syllables are stressed in accordance with the traditional rules of English accent—místress, nóthing—while monosyllabic words are stressed or unstressed relative to the words around them: "eyes" is stressed more strongly than "are" and the final syllable of "mistress," while "the" receives less emphasis than "like" and "sun." Notice also that long vowel sounds often coincide with stressed syllables ("eyes," "like"), but not necessarily ("my"). Indeed, the English iambic pentameter is a more flexible rhythm than is often assumed, and poets routinely reverse the stress pattern in one of the feet, producing a trochee (– ◡) instead of an iamb (◡ –). The most common position for such an inversion is the beginning of the line, where it is often subtle:

Why is my verse so barren of new pride

or

O, how I faint when I of you do write.

But inversion can be quite effective elsewhere as well:

Shall I compare **thee to** a summer's day?
‿ – | ‿ – | – ‿ | ‿ – | ‿ –

Further, stress can vary in degree even among accented syllables, producing rhythmic nuances within an overarching metrical scheme.[2]

Much medieval English poetry was based upon patterns of alliteration. "Alliterative meter," as it is called, typically occurs in a line with four heavily stressed syllables (which coincide with long vowel sounds) and a flexible number of other syllables in various possible combinations. The line is divided in two by a strong pause or "caesura" (see Section IV below), with the requirement that there be alliteration of one or two accented syllables in the first hemistich (or half-line) with the first accented syllable in the second hemistich.

The Anglo-Saxon epic "The Seafarer" was composed in the alliterative meter:

>   Þæt se mon ne wat
> Þe him on foldon   fægrost limpeð
> hu ic earmcearig   iscealdne sæ
> winter wunade   wræccan lastum,
> winemægum bidroren,
> bihongen hrimgocelum (12–17).

This poem was translated by Ezra Pound, who beautifully captured the sound and alliterative structure of the original:

>   Lest man know not
> That he on dry **land** // **loveliest** liveth,
> List how **I**, care-wretched, // on **ice**-cold sea,
> **Weathered** the **winter**, // **wretched** outcast
> Deprived of my kinsmen.[3]

The meters of classical Latin poetry are based upon an entirely different principle: "vowel quantity," or the time it takes to pronounce each syllable. In Latin as in

---

[2] This principle is lucidly demonstrated by Robert Pinsky, whose *Sounds of Poetry* is useful reading for the Latinist despite its English language focus.

[3] A more literal translation is: "He who happens pleasantly to be on dry land does not fully know how I passed a miserable winter on the ice-cold sea, on exile tracks, deprived of my kinsmen." Pound's version, however, is remarkable for its successful application of the Anglo-Saxon alliterative meter to modern English poetry.

English, some vowels are naturally long and others are naturally short, e.g., the English cǎp and cāpe, and the Latin *păter* and *māter*.[4] Syllables with short vowel sounds require less time to pronounce than syllables with long vowel sounds. Thus, *pŏpulus* (people) can be said more rapidly than *pōpulus* (poplar tree). Similarly, syllables ending with a vowel require less time to pronounce than syllables ending with a vowel plus one or more consonants. In accordance with these principles, the systematic alternation of long and short syllables determines the metrical pattern of a Latin poem. The first line of Vergil's *Aeneid*, for instance, has the following rhythm:

árma uirúmque canó Troíaé quí prímus ab óris

‒ ◡ ◡ ‒ ◡ ◡ ‒ ‒ ‒ ‒ ‒ ◡ ◡ ‒ ‒

It must be emphasized that accent has no bearing whatsoever on quantity in Latin verse. If it did, the same Vergilian line would have an entirely different poetic rhythm:

árma uirúmque cáno Troíae quí prímus áb óris.

Indeed, the Roman poets believed that varying the coincidence and divergence of quantity and quality, i.e. of the length and stress of vowels, was (within certain parameters to be discussed later) one of the artistic principles governing verse composition.

The Romans' use of a quantitative meter owes much to their admiration for and imitation and adaptation of Greek poetry, which is also based upon quantitative metrics. For the Greeks, poetry, music, and dance comprised a unified artistic endeavor in which the rhythms of the words were coordinated both with the rhythms of the music and with the dance steps. The attack and release of accent, the duration of tones, the rise and fall of pitch, and the rise and fall of the dancing foot were all organically intertwined. By Roman times, this nexus had been largely lost (although the degree of that loss is the subject of some debate), yet the poets retained much of the metrical structure of Greek poetry even when it was at odds with the natural practices of spoken Latin. As a result, Latin poetry, like, but perhaps more so than other poetries, was a highly stylized literary creation whose fundamental rules must be carefully observed by any modern poet who wishes to imitate the ancients faithfully.

---

[4] The student of Latin verse has little choice but to begin committing these to memory and reinforcing the skill by speaking and reading with correct pronunciation.

SECTION II: GENERAL RULES FOR DETERMINING THE QUANTITY OF SYLLABLES

The basic principle for determining the quantity of syllables in verse is simple and has been stated concisely by M.L. West: "A syllable is long if it is 'closed' (i.e. ends with a consonant), or if it contains a long vowel or diphthong. Otherwise it is short."[5] The application of this principle, however, is somewhat more difficult. If a single consonant follows a naturally short vowel (e.g., the *n* in *bonus*), that consonant tends to be attracted in speech to the *following* vowel, leaving the *preceding* syllable open and short (bŏ-nus). If, however, a syllable ends with a single consonant and the next syllable begins with another consonant (e.g., mul-tus), the first consonant tends to remain attracted to its *preceding* vowel, leaving the syllable closed or long (mūl-tus). In practice, then, it often takes *two* consonants to close or lengthen a syllable, but exceptions are numerous, and the following guidelines should be observed.

1. Vowels that are naturally long remain long in verse.

2. Diphthongs (two vowels that combine to make a single sound) are almost always long. Exception: the *ae* of the prefix *prae-* is generally shortened in verse before a following vowel, e.g., *stipitibus duris agitur sudibusue praeustis*, Vergil, *A.* 7.524 (see *correption[6]); more rarely, it is joined into a single syllable with the following vowel, e.g., *omnibus his Thesei dulcem praeoptarit amorem*, Cat. 64.120 (see *synizesis).

3. Vowels before other vowels are generally short, e.g., *at pius Aeneas per noctem plurima uoluens, A.* 1.305. Some notable exceptions: the genitive singular ending of the fifth declension is usually *-ēi*; the *i* of *fio* is long except before *er*; certain Greek words retain a naturally long vowel, e.g., aer, Eos; the *e* of the suffix *-eus* is sometimes long; the *i* of the genitive singular ending *-ius* may be long or short at the discretion of the poet, e.g., *nauibus (infandum!) amissis, unius ob iram (A.* 1.251), but *unius in miseri exitium conuersa tulere* (2.131).[7]

---

[5] *Greek Metre* (Oxford: Clarendon Press, 1982) 8.

[6] Words marked with an asterisk appear in the Glossary.

[7] For further exceptions and exceptions to the exceptions, see Postgate, *Prosodia Latina* (Oxford: Clarendon Press, 1923) 22–26.

5

4. A vowel followed by two consonants or a double consonant (*x* and *z*, which represent the sounds *ks* and *dz* or *zd*)[8] is generally long. Exception: a short vowel followed by a mute (*b, c, d, g, k, p, q, t*) and a liquid (*l, m, n, r) in the same syllable* may remain short or be lengthened at the discretion of the poet. Thus, *par levibus ventis vol**u**crique simillima somno, A.* 6.702, but *cum tacet omnis ager pecudes pictaeque vol**u**cres*, 4.525. When the two consonants are in two different syllables, the vowel must be long, e.g., *incute vim ventis submersasque* **obrue** *puppes, A.* 1.69, because the verb is *ob-ruo*, not *o-bruo*.

5. The final syllable of a word ending in a vowel and a single consonant is lengthened if the next word begins with a consonant, e.g., *Daedalus **ut** fama est fugiens Minoia regna (A.* 6.14).

6. But a short, open vowel at the end of a word is generally not lengthened if the next word begins with two consonants, no matter whether those two consonants are a mute/liquid combination, e.g., *illic res Italas Romanorumque* **triumphos**, *A.* 8.626, or not, e.g., *laetitia ludisque viae plausuque* **fremebant**, 8.717. Exceptions: the initial consonant combinations *sc-, sm-, sp-, sq-, st-*, and the double consonant *z* (and *zm-*) generally will not admit a preceding short final vowel, but (following Greek practice) the short is occasionally allowed to stand, e.g., *iam medio adparet fluctu nemorosa **Z**acynthos, A.* 3.270 and *tu poteras fragiles pinnis hebetare **z**maragdos*, Ov. *Am.* 2.6.21. Vergil even admits variation in lengthening within the same line: *terrasque **tr**actusque maris caelumque profundum, Ecl.* 4.51.[9]

7. A final vowel or diphthong or a final *m* with its preceding vowel is elided, or "struck out," by a vowel at the start of the next word, e.g., *conticuer(e) omnes intentique ora tenebant, A.* 2.1, and *et breuiter Troiae suprem(um) audire laborem*, 2.11.

8. The letter *h* is an aspirate and therefore does not count as a lengthening consonant, e.g., *sed cadat ante diem, mediaque inhumatus harena, A.* 4.620, nor does it preclude an elision, e.g., *nec plura his. ille admirans uenerabile donum*, 6.408.

---

[8] For purposes of syllabification, *x* and *z* tend to be attracted to their preceding vowels, e.g., sax-um, gaz-a.

[9] It must be noted, however, that this lengthening of *-que* may also be explained by two other considerations: the not uncommon practice of lengthening a syllable in arsis (see *arsis), and the fact that lengthening the initial *-que* in a *-que . . . -que* construction imitates Homer's lengthening of the initial τε in τε . . . τε constructions. These principles would also explain *Brontesque Steropesque et nudus membra Pyragmon* (*A.* 8.425), the only instance in Vergil in which an initial *st-* lengthens a final short vowel. For more on the lengthening of *-que*, see Section V.5.

EXERCISE I: VOWEL QUANTITY

Mark the naturally long (–) and short (⌣) vowels in the following common Latin words. Use a dictionary if necessary.

1. acies
2. aequor, aequoris
3. ago, agere
4. alienus
5. alius
6. amor, amoris
7. anima
8. ara
9. ater
10. caput, capitis
11. casus
12. clamor, clamoris
13. comes, comitis
14. cura
15. dea
16. dico, dicere
17. dies, diei
18. eripio, eripere
19. facio, facere
20. fatum
21. finis
22. futurus
23. geminus
24. genitor, genitoris
25. genus, generis

26. habeo, habere
27. honos, honoris
28. Italia
29. Italus
30. iubeo, iubere
31. labor, laboris
32. limen, liminis
33. litus, litoris
34. lumen, luminis
35. maneo, manere
36. mare
37. mater, matris
38. medius
39. meus
40. miser
41. munus, muneris
42. nauis
43. nomen, nominis
44. numen, numinis
45. oculus
46. os, oris
47. pater, patris
48. pelagus
49. pius
50. poena

51. primus
52. puer
53. refero
54. regina
55. res, rei
56. sacer
57. sedes, sedis
58. sidus, sideris
59. simul
60. socius
61. solus
62. super
63. talis
64. telum
65. totus
66. uates
67. uelum
68. uenio, uenire
69. uideo, uidere
70. uir
71. uires
72. uita
73. uoco, uocare
74. uolo, uelle
75. uolo, uolare

EXERCISE II: VOWEL QUANTITY

Mark all vowels that are either naturally long or lengthened according to the rules in section two above. Use a dictionary if necessary.

1. abripio, abripere
2. abstineo, abstinere
3. acerbus
4. admoueo, admouere
5. aggredior
6. agmen, agminis
7. alloquor
8. anhelus
9. antiquus
10. apertus
11. arcanus
12. artifex, artificis
13. atrox, atrocis
14. bellatrix
15. benignus
16. carmen, carminis
17. certamen, certaminis
18. concilium
19. corpus, corporis
20. defendo, defendere
21. difficilis
22. diuersus
23. euentus
24. excutio
25. fortuna

26. genetrix
27. germanus
28. gubernator
29. harundo, harundinis
30. horridus
31. ignotus
32. imperator
33. imperium
34. incipio, incipere
35. infelix, infelicis
36. lacertus
37. lacrima
38. lentus
39. libellus
40. magister
41. maximus
42. mortalis
43. mucro, mucronis
44. nefandus
45. obscurus
46. obsideo, obsidere
47. omnipotens
48. patria
49. perfectus
50. peruenio, peruenire

51. phalanx, phalangis
52. potens, potentis
53. puella
54. purpureus
55. relictus
56. repello, repellere
57. sanguis, sanguinis
58. secundus
59. sententia
60. sepulcrum
61. supplicium
62. supremus
63. suspicio, suspicere
64. tempestas, tempestatis
65. templum
66. tempus, temporis
67. totiens
68. tridens, tridentis
69. tumultus
70. turbidus
71. uerbum
72. ultimus
73. umbra
74. uoluptas, uoluptatis
75. uulnus, uulneris

SECTION III: THE DACTYLIC HEXAMETER

The dactylic hexameter is by far the most common and versatile of all Latin meters. Traditionally, it is the meter of *epic, *didactic, and *pastoral poetry, and it is often associated with serious and dignified themes, but it is also used for *satire. Modern practice, however, is less restrictive, and the hexameter is frequently used in translations of English poems or original poems on any subject.

The dactyl is a metrical unit or "foot" consisting of one long syllable followed by two short syllables (– ◡ ◡). It takes its name from the Greek word δάκτυλος, or "finger," because the finger has one long bone followed by two short bones. The term hexameter means "six measures" or "feet," so the dactylic hexameter is a line of verse consisting of six dactyls. In poetic time, which does not necessarily correspond to the time of normal speech, one long syllable lasts exactly twice as long as two short syllables. Therefore, it is permissible to substitute one long syllable for the two shorts of a dactyl, producing a spondee (– –).[10] Such substitutions are not uncommon in the first four feet of the line but avoided in the fifth foot, unless some special effect is desired. The sixth foot is never a dactyl; it is either a spondee or a trochee (– ◡). According to some metricians, the sixth foot is always spondaic, with any naturally short final syllable lengthened by virtue of its position at the end of the line. Other authorities regard a trochaic sixth foot as evidence of a catalectic, or "shortened," hexameter line. Whatever the case, the basic pattern of the dactylic hexameter may be schematized as follows:

$$- \overset{\smile\smile}{} \mid - \overset{\smile\smile}{} \mid - \overset{\smile\smile}{} \mid - \overset{\smile\smile}{} \mid - \overset{\smile\smile}{} \mid - \overset{\smile}{}$$

---

[10] The spondee takes its name from the Greek word σπονδή, "a libation," because wine-offerings to the gods were typically accompanied by poetry with spondaic rhythms. L.P. Wilkinson, *Golden Latin Artistry* (Cambridge, 1963) 61 cites a spondaic fragment of Terpander as evidence of the connection and notes that the Greeks found this rhythm appropriate to the occasion of a sacrifice "because of the solemnity of slowness and because the smooth regularity reflected the act of pouring."

EXERCISE III: THE HEXAMETER IN ENGLISH

The dactylic rhythm is rather difficult to achieve in English, which more readily lends itself to the iamb, but there have been some notable successes. In 1847, a group of poets collaborated on a project of *English Hexameter Translations*.[11] Dr. Thomas Hawtrey, a minor poet but technically skilled versifier, selected a passage from Book Three of Homer's *Iliad*. To get the feel of the hexameter rhythm, try to mark the accented syllables and foot divisions in this excerpt from Hawtrey's translation, which Matthew Arnold praised as "the most successful attempt hereto made at rendering Homer into English."[12]

> Clearly the rest I behold of the dark-ey'd sons of Achaia;
>
> Known to me well are the faces of all; their names I remember;
>
> Two, two only remain, whom I see not among the commanders,
>
> Kastor fleet in the car – Polydeukes brave with the cestus –
>
> Own dear brethren of mine – one parent loved us as infants.
>
> Are they not here in the host, from the shores of lov'd Lakedaimon?
>
> Or, tho' they came with the rest in the ships that bound thro' the waters,
>
> Dare they not enter the fight or stand in the council of Heroes,
>
> All for the fear of the shame and the taunts my crime has awaken'd?
>
> So said she; – they long since in Earth's soft arms were reposing,
>
> There, in their own dear land, their Father-land, Lakedaimon.

---

[11] *English Hexameter Translations* (London, 1847) 242.

[12] "On Translating Homer," Lecture III, *The Works of Matthew Arnold* (London: Macmillan, 1903) v. 5, 230.

EXERCISE IV: SCANSION, NO ELISIONS

The Latin hexameter follows the same basic pattern but relies upon vowel quantity rather than accent to determine the short and long syllables. Using the rules you have learned so far, mark the short and long syllables and foot divisions in the following lines from Vergil's *Aeneid*. There are no elisions (see Section II, 6–7).

1. ocius adducto torquens hastile lacerto
2. suspiciens altam Lunam sic uoce precatur
3. tu dea tu praesens nostro succurre labori
4. astrorum decus et nemorum Latonia custos
5. at tuba terribilem sonitum procul aere canoro
6. increpuit sequitur clamor caelumque remugit
7. accelerant acta pariter testudine Volsci
8. et fossas implere parant ac uellere uallum
9. hic Mars armipotens animum uiresque Latinis
10. addidit et stimulos acris sub pectore uertit
11. immisitque Fugam Teucris atrumque Timorem
12. dixerat ille rudem nodis et cortice crudo
13. intorquet summis adnixus uiribus hastam
14. haud aliter retro dubius uestigia Turnus
15. improperata refert et mens exaestuat ira
16. et iam Fama volans tanti praenuntia luctus
17. magna tropaea ferunt quos dat tua dextera Leto
18. tu quoque nunc stares immanis truncus in annis
19. esset par aetas et idem si robur ab annis
20. Turne sed infelix Teucros quid demoror armis
21. conditur in tenebras altum caligine caelum
22. spargitur et tellus lacrimis sparguntur et arma
23. it caelo clamorque virum clangorque tubarum
24. nec numero nec honore cremant tunc undique uasti
25. certatim crebris conlucent ignibus agri

EXERCISE V: SCANSION, ELISIONS

Scan the following lines from *Aeneid* 5, marking all syllables and foot divisions. Note that elisions do occur in the passage and that some lines contain more than one elision.

interea medium Aeneas iam classe tenebat

certus iter fluctusque atros Aquilone secabat

moenia respiciens quae iam infelicis Elissae

conlucent flammis quae tantum accenderit ignem

causa latet duri magno sed amore dolores

polluto notumque furens quid femina possit

triste per augurium Teucrorum pectora ducunt

ut pelagus tenuere rates nec iam amplius ulla

occurrit tellus maria undique et undique caelum

olli caeruleus supra caput adstitit imber

noctem hiememque ferens et inhorruit unda tenebris

ipse gubernator puppi Palinurus ab alta

heu quianam tanti cinxerunt aethera nimbi

quidue pater Neptune paras sic deinde locutus

colligere arma iubet ualidisque incumbere remis

obliquatque sinus in uentum ac talia fatur

magnanime Aenea non si mihi Iuppiter auctor

spondeat hoc sperem Italiam contingere caelo

mutati transuersa fremunt et uespere ab atro

consurgunt uenti atque in nubem cogitur aer

EXERCISE VI: SCANSION, PROPER NAMES

The following lines from *Aeneid* 7 contain only two elisions but include many difficult proper names. First, use your knowledge of the hexameter rhythm to try to reason out the scansion on your own. Then look up any unfamiliar words to complete the exercise.

hinc Agamemnonius Troiani nominis hostis

curru iungit Halaesus equos Turnoque ferocis

mille rapit populos uertunt felicia Baccho

Massica qui rastris et quos de collibus altis

Aurunci misere patres Sidicinaque iuxta

aequora quique Cales linquunt, amnisque uadosi

accola Volturni pariterque Saticulus asper

Oscorumque manus Teretes sunt aclydes illis

tela sed haec lento mos est aptare flagello

laeuas caetra tegit falcati comminus enses

nec tu carminibus nostris indictus abibis

Oebale quem generasse Telon Sebethide nympha

fertur Teleboum Capreas cum regna teneret

iam senior patriis sed non et filius aruis

contentus late iam tum dicione premebat

Sarrastis populos et quae rigat aequora Sarnus

quique Rufras Batulumque tenent atque arua Celemnae

et quos maliferae despectant moenia Abellae

Teutonico ritu soliti torquere cateias

tegmina quis capitum raptus de subere cortex

aerataeque micant peltae micat aereus ensis

SECTION IV: THE CAESURA

The term caesura (literally "a cutting") has two different but interrelated meanings. On the one hand, it refers to a slight rhythmic pause or break in a line of verse, often corresponding with a syntactic break, i.e. the end of a phrase, clause, or sentence. Designated by the symbol ‖, the caesura falls after the word "clear" in this famous line of Pope:

One truth is clear, ‖ whatever is, is right,

and after "ledge" in this hexameter line from Kingsley's *Andromeda*:

Slowly she went by the ledge; ‖ and the maid was alone in the darkness,

and after "pedes" in Vergil's

Quo te, Moeri, pedes? ‖ an, quo uia ducit, in urbem?

On the other hand, the term caesura also refers specifically to a break between words within a metrical foot and as such is opposed to *diaresis, the coincidence of word and foot endings. In this sense, the Vergilian line quoted above has not one but five caesurae, while diaresis (indicated by the symbol ⋮) occurs four times:

quo ‖ te ⋮ Moeri ‖ pedes? ‖ an ⋮ quo ‖ uia ⋮ ducit ‖ in ⋮ urbem?

When the caesura follows a short syllable (*Moeri, ducit*), it is called "weak." When it follows a long syllable (*quo, pedes, quo*), it is called "strong."[13]

The Greeks and Romans believed that the variation of caesura and diaresis was central to the poet's rhythmic artistry, and lines with no caesurae, like Ennius's

sparsis ⋮ hastis ⋮ longis ⋮ campus ⋮ splendet et horret,

---

[13] The terms "masculine" and "feminine" are sometimes used to describe "strong" and "weak" caesurae.

were generally avoided. Indeed, every hexameter should have at least one strong caesura somewhere near the middle of the line. This "main caesura" typically occurs either after two-and-a-half feet (called "penthemimeral," i.e. after five half-feet) or after three-and-a-half feet (called "hephthemimeral," i.e. after seven half-feet). The penthemimeral caesura is somewhat more common, and if a hephthemimeral caesura is used, it is often, but not necessarily, balanced by a strong caesura in the second foot.

The opening lines of Vergil's first *Georgic* provide a fine example of the poet's varied use of strong caesurae:

Quid faciat ‖ laetas segetes, ‖ quo sidere terram
uertere, Maecenas, ‖ ulmisque adiungere uitis
conueniat, ‖ quae cura boum, ‖ qui cultus habendo
sit pecori, ‖ apibus ‖ quanta experientia parcis,
hinc canere incipiam. ‖

In the first line, the poet employs a hephthemimeral caesura balanced by a caesura in the second foot but one that is not strongly felt syntactically. In the second line, he switches to the penthemimeral caesura, while the third line has strong and syntactically marked caesurae in the second and fourth feet. In the fourth line there is a strong caesura in the third foot, but it is the second foot caesura that is syntactically more pronounced,[14] and the fourth foot caesura is obscured by elision. Then in the fifth line, there is a strong, sentence-ending penthemimeral caesura.

Vergil also felt free to make ample use of weak caesurae, especially when he was striving for a Greek effect.[15] In general, a weak caesura in the third foot is compensated by a strong caesura in the fourth foot (and often in the second as well). Thus,

formosam ‖ resonare ‖ doces ‖ Amaryllida siluas (*E.* 1.5).

The presence of a strong caesura in the fourth foot, however, should not dissuade us from regarding a weak caesura in the third foot as the main caesura, if syntax so suggests, as in,

O crudelis Alexi, ‖ nihil mea carmina curas? (*E.* 2.6).

---

[14] For the *hiatus, or failure to have an elision where one is expected, see Section V.2.
[15] Weak caesurae in the hexameter seem "Greek" because they were regularly used by Homer.

EXERCISE VII: CAESURA AND DIARESIS

Scan the following lines from Vergil, marking each caesura and diaresis. Use the following symbols: ‖ for the main caesura(e), | for other caesurae, and ⋮ for diaresis.

Nec minus et miseri diuersa in parte Latini

innumeras struxere pyras, et corpora partim

multa uirum terrae infodiunt auectaque partim

finitimos tollunt in agros urbique remittunt,

cetera confusaeque ingentem caedis aceruum

nec numero nec honore cremant: tunc undique uasti

certatim crebris conlucent ignibus agri.

tertia lux gelidam caelo dimouerat umbram:

maerentes altum cinerem et confusa ruebant

ossa focis tepidoque onerabant aggere terrae.

Iam uero in tectis, praediuitis urbe Latini,

praecipuus fragor et longi pars maxima luctus.

Hic matres miseraeque nurus, hic cara sororum

pectora maerentum puerique parentibus orbi

durum exsecrantur bellum Turnique hymenaeos:

ipsum armis ipsumque iubent decernere ferro,

qui regnum Italiae et primos sibi poscat honores.

ingrauat haec saeuus Drances solumque uocari

testatur, solum posci in certamina Turnum.

Multa simul contra uariis sententia dictis

pro Turno, et magnum reginae nomen obumbrat,

multa uirum meritis sustentat fama tropaeis.

SECTION V: VARIATIONS AND IRREGULARITIES

One occasionally finds in the vast body of classical Latin hexameters apparent departures from the rules learned thus far. Such metrical irregularities, if used sparingly and judiciously, can serve a valid poetic purpose, either by providing some special, meaningful rhythmic effect or by simply lending a pleasantly creative variety to the verse. Moreover, the careful application of unusual metrical effects can be a vital part of the successful imitation of the ancient poets. Some caution is called for, however. No Roman poet has metrical fireworks in every other line, and the imprudent use of unusual rhythms will produce a sloppy and undisciplined imitation of the classical models and, worse, a verse that is pointlessly choppy and inelegant. A good rule of thumb is this: If a metrical variant has a precedent[16] in one or more ancient authors *and* if its presence adds something significant to the poem, its use is justified. Whatever fails to meet both of these criteria should be avoided. The paragraphs below review some of the most important metrical anomalies.

1. Elision at the caesura. Elision at the caesura occurs when the caesura immediately follows an elided vowel. In one sense, this is perfectly proper. Since the vowel is elided, it is disregarded in the scansion of the line, which is then correctly divided by the caesura. In the practice of recitation, however, elided vowels were probably lightly sounded. This situation presents something of a dilemma. If the elided vowel is sounded before the pause, the caesura is weakened, and if it is reserved until after the pause, it becomes detached from the word to which it semantically belongs. Therefore, elision at the penthemimeral caesura is generally avoided unless compensated by a proper hephthemimeral caesura, and vice versa. Lines such as

his dictis ‖ impens(o) | animum ‖ flammauit amore (*A.* 4.54)

and

hinc fore ductores, ‖ reuocat(o) | a sanguine Teucri (*A.* 1.235),

---

[16] M. Platnauer, *Latin Elegiac Verse* (Cambridge: Cambridge UP, 1951) and S. E. Winbolt, *Latin Hexameter Verse* (London: Methuen, 1903) provide detailed information about what does and does not occur in classical Latin verse. They are essential reference books for any modern Latin poet.

in which the elision does not occur at the *main* caesura, are not uncommon. The elision of -*que* at the penthemimeral caesura is also not unusual in Vergil, even if there is no hephthemimeral caesura:

 ossa focis tepido(que) ‖ onerabant aggere terrae (*A.* 11.212).

Elision of anything other than -*que* at the penthemimeral caesura without a proper hephthemimeral caesura is either rare or non-existent; I have not yet found an example.

2. The opposite phenomenon is hiatus at the caesura. Hiatus takes place when an expected elision of a long vowel fails to occur. Typically, hiatus corresponds with a sense break, e.g.,

 posthabita coluisse Samo: ‖ hic illius arma (*A.* 1.16)

and

 antiqua e cedro, ‖ Italusque paterque Sabinus (*A.* 7.178),

but not necessarily:

 quid struit? aut qua spe ‖ inimica . . . (*A.* 4.235).

Hiatus is also found in the first, second, and fifth foot caesurae:

 o | utinam . . . (*Am.* 2.5.7)[17]
 sit pecori, | apibus . . . (*G.* 1.4)
 euolat infelix et femineo | ululatu (*A.* 4.667)
 . . . Dardani**o** | Anchisae (*A.* 1.617).

Hiatus very rarely occurs at a diaresis, but a foot-ending long vowel may be shortened. This phenomenon is called correption, and it is almost always used as an imitation of Greek practice.

 uictor apud rapidum Simoenta sub Ilio alto (*A.* 5.261).

---

[17] This hiatus is very common. Indeed, the interjections *o*, *a*, and *heu* rarely, if ever, elide; I have not yet found an example and do not expect to.

Correption may also occur at a weak caesura, e.g.,

credimus? an qui amant ipsi sibi somnia fingunt? (*E.* 8.108).

It is, of course, metrically impossible to have correption at a strong caesura since a vowel preceding such a pause must, be definition, be long. Vergil was among the boldest and most creative users of hiatus and correption, and *Georgics* 1.437 is particularly remarkable:

Glauco et Panopeae et Inoo Melicertae.

There is a hiatus after the first foot (unprecedented in Latin), and correption occurs at the weak caesura in the third foot. Similarly, in *Eclogue* 6, the poet daringly allows "Hyla" to have two different prosodies in the same line, with hiatus at the penthemimeral caesura and correption at the end of the fourth foot:

clamassent, ut litus 'Hyla Hyla' omne sonaret (44).

3. Other unusual caesurae. While weak caesurae are not uncommon, it is somewhat unusual to find one in the third foot if there is no strong hephthemimeral caesura in the line. In Vergil's

permixtos heroas ‖ et ipse uidebitur illis (*E.* 4.16),

the fourth foot caesura is weak, and in Ovid's

Irus egens pecorisque ‖ Melanthius auctor edendi (*Her.* 1.95),

there is no fourth foot caesura at all. Such lines are rare, but they do occur. In addition, a word break at the end of the second foot was considered an inelegant interference with the penthemimeral caesura, presumably because a one-syllable word before the caesura would make the line seem choppy, and a two-syllable word would make the caesura weak. Accordingly, second foot diaresis is rare, and when it occurs there is usually a strong caesura in the fourth foot, as in

praecipuus ‖ fragor ⁞ et longi ‖ pars maxima luctus (*A.* 11.214).

Indeed, it was considered so odious for diaresis to fall a half-foot before an expected caesura that the presence of word breaks at the ends of both the first and second feet in line 113 of the *Epistula Sapphus* — postquam ⋮ se dolor ⋮ inuenit, nec pectora plangi — has led many to suspect that Ovid could not have written it.

4. Synizesis occurs when two consecutive vowels that do not naturally form a Latin diphthong are joined into a single syllable. In some cases, synizesis is the result of a tendency in speech for two similar vowels to be combined into a single sound. Synizesis is particularly common with prepositional prefixes ending in *-e*, e.g., *non liquidi gregibus fontes, non gramina deerunt* (*G.* 2.200), *tu patrui meritas conare anteire secures* (Prop. 1.6.19), and *quid deinde rogabo?* (*M.* 3.465);[18] the initial *ea-* and *eo-* of *eadem* and *eodem*, e.g., *haec eadem docuit, 'cuium pecus, an Meliboei?'* (*E.* 5.87) and *hoc eodem ferro stillet uterque cruor* (Prop. 2.8.26); and words ending in *-ea* and *-eo*, e.g., *ipse deus uatum palla spectabilis aurea* (Ov. *Am.* 1.8.59) and *hic finis fandi. solio tum Iuppiter aureo* (*A.* 10.116).[19] Synizesis is also common in the *eu* and *ei* and *ea* of Greek proper names, e.g., Orpheus, Orpheu, Orphei, Orphea (*G.* 4.454, 496, 545; *E.* 6.30). When the first vowel is an *i* or a *u*, it can become semi-consonantal in synizesis, e.g., *Italiam fato profugus Lauiniaque uenit* (*A.* 1.2)[20] or *genua labant, uastos quatit aeger anhelitus artus* (5.432). The opposite of synizesis is vocalic diaeresis, in which a consonantal *u* is transformed into a vowel, especially in forms of *soluo* and *uoluo*, e.g., *persoluenda* (*Her.* 6.74) and *euoluisse* (12.4).

5. Lengthening of vowels. The final syllable of a word ending in a naturally short vowel plus a single consonant (e.g., domŭs) generally remains short if the next word begins with a vowel, e.g., *hic domus Aeneae cunctis dominabitur oris* (*A.* 3.97). That final syllable, however, is sometimes lengthened when it falls at the caesura, e.g., *et direpta domus, et parui casus Iuli* (*A.* 2.563). Lengthening at the hephthemimeral caesura also occurs, e.g., *cum sic Mercurium adloquitur ac talia mandat* (*A.* 4.222). Typically, vowels are only lengthened at a *main* caesura, but Vergil daringly extends the principle to the fifth-foot caesura in his sixth *Eclogue: ille latus niueum molli fultus hyacintho* (53). Ovid is particularly fond of lengthening the second *i* of the third person singular perfect indicative of *eo* and its compounds, e.g., *nec, quae praeteriit, iterum reuocabitur unda* (*AA.* 3.63). Aside from this lengthening before *t*, which is perhaps less an irregularity than a reflection of

---

[18] The synizesis of the *ei* in *deinde* occurs so frequently as to be the norm.

[19] The effect is the same in lines such as *A.* 5.269, *puniceis ibant euincti tempora taenis* and 6.653, *per campum pascuntur equi. quae gratia currum*, in which *taenis* and *currum* are the contracted forms of *taeniis* and *curruum*.

[20] Some editors print "Lauinaque," but the synizesis of *ia* finds parallels at *A.* 6.33 (*quin protinus omnia*) and 7.237 (*uerba precantia*); moreover, "Lauiniaque" is better Latin. Cf. also *A.* 2.16, *intexunt abiete costas.*

an older quantity,[21] lengthening is most likely to occur before *l, m, n, r*, or *s*.[22] Although a short final vowel is generally not lengthened before a word beginning with two consonants, there are exceptions. Short open vowels are generally not placed before words beginning with *sc, sm, sp,* or *st*, but when they do occur before these consonant combinations, lengthening is subject to the following rules: If the vowel falls in the first half of the foot (and therefore before a caesura, even if not a main caesura), it is often lengthened, e.g., *nulla fugae ratio, nulla spes: omnia muta* (Cat. 64.186). When the vowel falls in the second half of the foot, it is generally short, e.g., *ponite. spes sibi quisque; sed haec quam angusta uidetis* (*A.* 11.309). The enclitic *-que* (particularly in *-que . . . -que* constructions) is often lengthened according to the same principles in order to imitate the lengthening of τε in Homer's τε . . . τε constructions, e.g., *Brontesque Steropesque et nudus membra Pyragmon* (*A.* 8.425). *-Que* can also be lengthened before other consonant combinations, e.g., *ensemque clipeumque et rubrae cornua cristae* (*A.* 12.89), or more daringly before a single consonant, e.g., *liminaque laurusque dei totusque moueri* (*A.* 3.91).[23] Short open vowels in the second half of a foot often remain short even when followed by three consonants, e.g., *linquimus, insani ridentes praemia scribae* (Horace, *Sat.* 1.5.35), and are quite commonly short before the word *zmaragdus*.

6. Shortening of vowels. A naturally long internal vowel or diphthong is often shortened when it falls before another vowel (or *h* plus a vowel). This practice is particularly common with the prefixes *de* and *prae*, e.g., *infindunt pariter sulcos, totumque dehiscit* (*A.* 5.142) and *stipitibus duris agitur sudibusue praeustis* (*A.* 7.525). Sometimes, however, the vowels are joined into a single syllable, e.g., *Eurum ad se Zephyrumque uocat, dehinc talia fatur* (*A.* 1.31) and *omnis his Thesei dulcem praeoptarit amorem* (Cat. 64.120). Final long vowels may be shortened before initial vowels, e.g., *nomen et arma locum seruant; te, amice, nequiui* (*A.* 6.507). [See section V.2 on hiatus and correption.] Horace, Propertius, Ovid, and later authors often shorten the final long *o* of first person singular verbs, especially (but not exclusively) words of two syllables, e.g., *credo, puto, rogo, scio, tollo, uolo*. The final *o* of proper names is often shortened as well, e.g., *Naso*. The shortening of other forms should be avoided unless intended as a specific imitation of later poets. The final vowels of *mihi, sibi, tibi, ubi,* and *modo* were originally long but are shortened so frequently as to be the norm. Tibullus cleverly scans *ubi* both ways in *Delos ubi nunc, Phoebe, tua est, ubi Delphica Pytho*? (2.3.27).

---

[21] Postgate 28–9.
[22] Postgate 29.
[23] Postgate 34 claims that only the single consonants *l, m, n, r,* and *s* are allowed to lengthen a *-que*, but he is forced to admit Ovidian exceptions, e.g., *telasque calathosque infectaque pensa reponunt* (*M.* 4.10).

7. Hypermetric lines. A hypermetric line is a line that goes *beyond* (hyper-) its standard hexameter *measure* (-metric). These lines are rare,[24] and in each case the extra syllable is able to be elided by a vowel at the start of the next line. Such an elision, in effect, returns the hypermetric line to its "normal" length. The possibility of an elision across a line break is not entirely different from an elision at the caesura and may result from a tendency in recitation not to make an exaggerated pause at the end of each line (especially if there is no sense break[25]) but to join successive lines fluidly together. It must be noted, however, that one should not expect an interlinear elision just because one line ends in a vowel and the next begins with one. Such vowel combinations, although rare in the lyric meters, are actually quite common in the hexameter (six in the first twenty lines of the *Aeneid*, for instance), and elision only occurs if the first line is hypermetric. In most cases the elided syllable is -*que*, a particle that is often elided elsewhere in the line. Vergil elides a hypermetric inflected ending only four times:

aut dulcis musti Volcano decoquit umorem
et foliis undam trepidi despumat aeni (*G.* 1.295–296)

inseritur uero et fetu nucis arbutus horrida,
et steriles platani malos gessere ualentis (*G.* 2.69–70)

et spumas miscent argenti uiuaque sulpura
Idaeasque pices et pinguis unguine ceras (*G.* 3.449–450)

iamque iter emensi turris ac tecta Latinorum
ardua cernebant iuuenes muroque subibant (*A.* 7.160–161).

<hr/>

[24] Friedrich Crusius, *Römische Metrik* (Munich: Max Hueber, 1955) 37 n.1 writes that there are "ungefähr 20" hypermetric lines in Vergil, but Papillon and Haigh, *Virgil* (Oxford: Clarendon Press, 1892) lv are right to claim that there are exactly twenty-two. Here they are: *Georgics* 1.295, 2.69, 2.344, 2.443, 3.242, 3.377, 3.449; *Aeneid* 1.332, 1.448, 2.745, 4.558, 4.629, 5.422, 5.753, 6.602, 7.160, 7.470, 8.228, 9.650, 10.781, 10.895, 11.609.

[25] Vergil daringly allows a hypermetric elision across a strong sense break five times: *G.* 2.443, *A.* 7.470, 10.895, and 4.629, which is also the end of a rather long speech by Dido:
"litora litoribus contraria, fluctibus undas
imprecor, arma armis; pugnent ipsique nepotes**que**."
haec ait, et partis animum uersabat in omnis,
inuisam quaerens quam primum abrumpere lucem.
Here the hypermetric elision allows the unending hatred of Dido's speech to bleed into the words of the narrator, effectively suggesting that her curse will extend beyond her death (just as the meter extends beyond her speech), while also vividly dramatizing the queen's agitation as she resolves to commit suicide "as soon as possible" (*quam primum*).

In some cases, hypermetric lines seem to be little more than a metrical convenience, but they are often used to good effect. A line running over its bounds may suggest the "bubbling over" of unfermented grape juice (*G.* 1.295, above), or an overhanging rock (*quos super atra silex iam iam lapsura cadentique / imminet adsimilis, A.* 6.602–3), or excited horses (*subito erumpunt clamore frementisque / exhortantur equos, A.* 11.609–10), or, more fancifully, the foaming scum that floats on top of molten silver ore (*G.* 3.449, above), and "wandering" past the end of a line (*ignari hominumque locorumque / erramus, A.* 1.332–333).

8. Other irregular line endings. In order to mark the ending of a hexameter line, it is customary to have a dactyl in the fifth foot and for the initial long syllables of the last two feet to coincide with their word accents, e.g., *saucia cura, ora tenebant,* and *primus ab oris* (*A.* 4.1, 2.1, 1.1) This principle holds true even when the penultimate word begins in the fourth foot, e.g., *euertere gentem* (*A.* 3.1). In addition, the final word typically has either two or three syllables. This pattern is occasionally violated by the poets, often (but not always) for some special effect. Irregular lines fall into four categories: 1) lines ending with a monosyllable, 2) lines ending with two disyllables, 3) quadrisyllabic and pentasyllabic endings, and 4) spondaic endings. A line ending in a monosyllable is likely to cause a conflict between vowel quantity and stress because the preceding word will generally have more than one long syllable and/or a long final syllable, which never receives an accent in Latin. A preceding choriamb ($- \cup \cup -$) has long syllables where accents cannot fall, e.g., *ilicibus sus* (*A.* 3.390 and 8.43), as does a preceding iamb ($\cup -$), e.g., *uirum quem* (*A.* 1.151), or a preceding anapest ($\cup \cup -$), e.g., *hominum rex* (*A.* 2.648). A line ending with two monosyllables may be similarly disruptive if they, in turn, are preceded by a pyrrhic ($\cup \cup$), whose first syllable is both short and accented. Furthermore, if the pyrrhic is itself preceded by a word of two or more syllables, the initial long syllable of the fifth foot will necessarily be unaccented. If, however, the pyrrhic is preceded by a monosyllable, e.g., *haec tibi mens est* (*A.* 8.400), or a trochee ($- \cup$) whose final syllable is elided, e.g., *his uocibus usa est* (*A.* 1.64), the harshness is arguably lessened. Nevertheless, a double monosyllabic ending should still be considered irregular even if quantity and accent coincide throughout, e.g., *numina, si quid* (*A.* 1.603). A line ending in two disyllables, e.g., *morae fuit Ilo* (*A.* 10.400), suffers the same problem as a line ending in a pyrrhic and two monosyllables, yet Vergil writes many such verses and generally takes care that the disyllables are preceded by a monosyllable, e.g., *o dea certe* (*A.* 1.328). Quadrisyllabic endings are metrically problematic for the same reason as endings of two disyllables: the conflict of stress and accent at the start of the fifth foot. Vergil has a particular fondness for the Greek words *hymenaeos* and *hyacinthus* and for Greek names, but more strictly Latinate endings are also possible, e.g., *comitatu* (*A.* 4.215). Often a quadrisyllabic ending

will combine with some other metrical effect such as hiatus, e.g., *ulla moram fecere, neque Aonie Aganippe* (*E.* 10.12), absence of a strong caesura, e.g., *Messapus Cloniumque Lycaoniumque Erichaeten* (*A.* 10.749), or a spondaic ending (see below), e.g., *proximus huic, longo sed proximus interuallo* (*A.* 5.320), used here with good effect to suggest the slowness of the lagging runner. It is, of course, possible to achieve coincidence of accent and quantity if the quadrisyllable is preceded by a monosyllable, e.g., *an Meliboei* (*E.* 5.87). Pentasyllabic endings are irregular because they have at least two long syllables but only one accent.[26] Such endings are generally reserved for Greek proper names, with or without a -*que*, e.g., Alphesiboeus, Pantagienque, Tauromenumque (*E.* 8.62; Ov. *Fast.* 4.471, 75), but are sometimes used for effect, e.g., *perfractaque quadrupedantum / pectora pectoribus rumpunt*, describing the violent collision of the horses of Tyrrhenus and Aconteus (*A.* 11.614–5). If the fifth foot consists of a spondee instead of a dactyl, the ending is said to be "spondaic," and the line is called a σπονδειάζων (*spondiadzon*). The final word generally consists of either three or four syllables, e.g., *narcisso, abscondantur* (*E.* 5.38, *G.* 1.221), and at least one of the first four feet (preferably the fourth) should be a dactyl.[27] Lines with no dactyls are extremely rare in Latin poetry, despite the Homeric precedents.[28] Ennius's six holospondaic lines (one of which is doubtful) appear to be the only extant examples.[29] While lines such as *olli respondit rex Albai Longai* (*Ann.* 31) nicely use the spondaic rhythm to convey the solemnity of the occasion described (in this case, the establishment of a treaty), Vergil seems to have been sufficiently averse to lines with no dactyls that he introduced one in the fifth foot when he adapted the Ennian line in *Aeneid* 12: *olli sedato respondit corde Latinus* (18).

---

[26] Winbolt 134 n.1 suggests that the presence of a secondary accent in words like *sollicitabant* may explain Lucretius's fondness for pentasyllables, but how strongly, if at all, such secondary accents were felt must remain a matter of speculation.

[27] Commenting on Catullus 64.3 (Aeetaeos) C. J. Fordyce observes that of the 30 σπονδιάζοντες of Catullus 64, only two (3, 44) have spondaic fourth feet.

[28] There are six holospondaic lines in Homer, *Il.* 2.544, 11.130, 23.221; *Od.* 15.334, 21.15, 22.175 (= 22.192), including the famous ψυχὴν κικλήσκων Πατροκλῆος δειλοῖο (*Il.* 23.221) describing the solemn funeral rites for Patroclus.

[29] O. Skutsch, *The Annals of Q. Ennius* (Oxford: Clarendon, 1985) 49 identifies 31, 117, 157, 190, 286, and *Dub.* vii.

SECTION VI: GREEK WORDS AND NAMES

The poets of ancient Rome, like all educated citizens of their day, were fluent in both Latin and Greek, and they were well-trained in Greek poetry, which the Romans self-consciously sought to perpetuate and adapt to Latin in matters of rhythm, style, and subject matter, if not language. It should therefore not be surprising that some Greek words and many Greek proper names made their way into Latin verse. The prosody of such words, and the metrical practices associated with them, may pose a challenge for the Latinist with little or no background in Greek, but it is well worth the effort. If handled appropriately, the inclusion of Greek words may form the basis of a meaningful literary or historical allusion, display the poet's learning, lend a pleasantly musical variety to a line, or simply add a bit of panache and sophistication to a poem, in much the same way as a well-placed *bon mot* in French may convey refinement to speakers of English.

When composing original poetry, all natural vowel quantities must be verified by consulting a good dictionary,[30] but two general principles may serve as a useful aid to scansion: 1) Vowels retain their original Greek quantity; often they will be short, even where one might expect a long vowel in Latin. 2) Greek words tend to attract unusual metrical features that are not so uncommon in Greek poetry. Let us take each in turn.

Short Vowels: Whereas Latin has approximately two long syllables for every short, Greek has approximately two shorts for every long, and many vowels that tend to be long in Latin are typically short in Greek: 1) υ — Although the Latin *u* is usually long, the Greek upsilon, υ, conventionally expressed in Latin as a *y*, is usually short. 2) *-i* — As a noun ending, *-i* is always long in Latin, but as a Greek vocative, *-i* is short (*Moeri*). 3) *-as* — The Latin ending *-as*, whether nominative singular (*libertas*), accusative plural (*poetas*), or part of an adverb (*cras*), is always long. In words borrowed from Greek, however, the ending *-as* is typically short (*heroas*). 4) *-os* — Similarly, the Latin ending *-os*, whether nominative singular (*custos*) or accusative plural (*agros*), is almost always long in Latin; *os* (bone) and *compos* ("having control of," formed from *con* and *potis*, which has a short *o*) are the only exceptions. As a Greek ending, *-os* is often short. 5) *-eus* — As the ending of Greek names in the nominative, *-eus* is scanned as a single syllable. 6) *E* and *O* — Greek has two *e*'s and two *o*'s; one of each is long (*η, ω*), the other short (*ε, o*).

---

[30] The *Chambers/Murray Latin-English Dictionary* (Larousse Kingfisher Chambers, 1992) has the benefit of including hidden long vowel markings.

When taken over into Latin, Greek words retain the quantity of their original vowels (*Eos, Laocoon*) or, conversely, the uncertainty of quantity (*Eous*).

Greek Rhythms: The presence of Greek words in a line will often prompt a Roman poet to employ metrical features characteristic of Greek poetry. Among the most commonly used are weak caesurae (quite frequent, indeed almost mandatory), polysyllabic endings, hiatus, correption, and unusual lengthening of vowels.

EXERCISE VIII: METRICAL ANOMALIES

The following lines contain various metrical anomalies. Some lines have three or four unusual metrical features. Scan each line and explain the irregularities.

Tityrus hinc aberat. ipsae te, Tityre, pinus

Amphion Dircaeus in Actaeo Aracyntho

addam cerea pruna (honos erit huic quoque pomo)

te Corydon, o Alexi: trahit sua quemque uoluptas

munera sunt lauri et suaue rubens hyacinthus

Orphei Calliopea, Lino formosus Apollo

pro molli uiola, pro purpureo narcisso

saltantis Satyros imitabitur Alphesiboeus

non iniussa cano. si quis tamen haec quoque si quis

ille latus niueum molli fultus hyacintho

uersibus ille facit aut si non possumus omnes

stant et iuniperi et castaneae hirsutae

ut uidi ut perii ut me malus abstulit error

ulla moram fecere neque Aonie Aganippe

omnia uincit Amor: et nos cedamus Amori

liquerat Ortygien Megereaque Pantagienque

perque urbes Asiae longum petit Hellespontum

neue recusarem, uerbis Iouis imperat et se

o utinam, Macareu, quae nos commisit in unum

ille Noto Zephyroque et Sithonio Aquiloni

Nisaee Spioque Thaliaque Cymodoceque

ingemuit Glaucumque Medontaque Thersilochumque

tris Antenoridas Cererique sacrum Polyboeten

atque Ephyre atque Opis et Asia Deiopea

atque Getae atque Hebrus et Actias Orithyia

SECTION VII: SOUND AND SENSE

> True ease in writing comes from art, not chance,
> As those move easiest who have learn'd to dance.
> 'Tis not enough no harshness gives offence,
> The sound must seem an Echo to the sense.
>
> — Alexander Pope, *An Essay on Criticism* 362–365

As the eminently quotable Pope reminds us, the dynamic interaction of sound and sense is central to the poet's art, whether it takes the form of outright onomatopoeia, or a more subtle reinforcement of the tone of a passage, or even an ironic contrast between sound and meaning. Pope demonstrates the principle in the lines that follow:

> But when loud surges lash the sounding shore,
> The hoarse, rough verse should like the torrent roar:
> When Ajax strives, some rock's vast weight to throw,
> The line too labours, and the words move slow (368–371).

The sound of splashing waves lapping against the shore is echoed in the alliteration of *l* and *s* and by the repetition of *s* and *sh* sounds in line 368, while line 369 reflects the harshness and power of the ocean with its irregular rhythm: instead of writing the smoothly iambic "the verses hoarse and rough like torrents roar," Pope roughens the rhythm by eliminating the conjunction between the adjectives, leaving the stressed "rough" in an unstressed position.[31] To capture the ponderous efforts of Ajax described in line 370, Pope strays again from the iambic pentameter in 371, ending each hemistich with three long, stressed syllables: $\cup - - - \cup \| \cup \cup - - -$.

These interpretations, and those that will follow, are assuredly both subjective and unverifiable, and it is not necessary for every reader to hear the same effects in every line. It is important, however, to observe how the particular sounds of individual words arranged in a particular order interact with the poem's general metrical pattern, and to reflect upon how that interaction affects the way one reads a poem. Nowhere are such effects more carefully studied than in Augustan poetry, and they fall into three broad categories: rhythm, consonant and vowel sounds, and the arrangement of words.

---

[31] Had Pope merely inverted the second foot, turning the iamb into a trochee, a stressed third syllable would have been an acceptable variation in the iambic pentameter, but "verse" is also stressed.

28

PART A: RHYTHM

It is often said that, as a general principle, dactyls convey swiftness, lightness, and excitement, while spondees convey slowness, heaviness, and solemnity. This claim may be a good place to start, but it does not take us very far apart from the consideration of particular lines. The exact same sequence of long and short syllables may have an entirely different effect when set to different words, especially if there are also differences in caesura and diaeresis. Moreover, rhythmic effects are arguably more pronounced the rarer they are. *Iliad* 1.1–35, for instance, has five entirely dactylic lines while there are none in the first thirty-five lines of the *Aeneid*. Even the relatively swift hexameters of Ovid's *M.* 1.1–35 lack holodactylic lines.[32] Thus, when Vergil writes,

ille uolat simul arua fuga simul aequora uerrens (*G.* 3.201),

describing the sweeping rush of the north wind, and

quadripedante putrem sonitu quatit ungula campum (*A.* 8.596),

imitating the rapid gallop of charging horses, the onomatopoetic effect stands out. On the other hand, the lightness of the dactyl can suggest gentleness and even languor, and Vergil uses a purely dactylic rhythm to illustrate the approach of sleep and death:

te, Palinure, petens tibi somnia tristia portans (*A.* 5.840).

Here the effect is enhanced by the presence of diaeresis after the third, fourth, and fifth feet and by the coincidence of stress and quantity in the last three words.

---

[32] The fact the Greek has roughly two short syllables for every long while Latin has roughly two longs for every short may partially account for this striking difference between Homer and Vergil. It is perhaps not too much of a fine point to note that Vergil appears to have had a stylistic fondness for the fourth foot spondee, even in an otherwise dactylic line. Similarly, when he reworks 8.596 in book 11 (*quadripedumque putrem cursu quatit ungula campum*, 875), he introduces a third-foot spondee, arguably without much reducing the galloping effect. Horace remarks that *spondei stabiles* ("steady," "stabilizing," or "stately" spondees) give slowness and weight to the iambic trimeter (*AP* 256), and perhaps Vergil desired this effect for his epic hexameters.

These features complement the dactylic beat to give the line-ending a tranquil and sleepy uniformity[33] that contrasts with the typical metrical dynamism of the hexameter. That these rhythms probably would have suggested sleep to a Roman ear is shown by lines such as,

> *luna premit suadentque cadentia sidera somnos* (*A.* 4.81[34]),

and

> *spargens umida mella soporiferumque papauer* (486),

which describe the onset of sleep, and in which dactyls predominate and accented syllables coincide with long vowels; notice also the repeated *s* sounds and the lack of a strong caesura in each.

If dactyls can suggest the effect of falling asleep, slow spondees can reflect the restful calm of sleep itself:

> *Aeneas celsa in puppi, iam certus eundi,*
> *carpebat somnos, rebus iam rite paratis* (*A.* 4.554–55).

Here the spondees are extended over two lines,[35] perhaps to underscore how Aeneas's peaceful repose contrasts with the sleepless agitation of Dido (522–553). Since spondees often convey solemnity as well, these lines may also prepare us for the hero's divine vision of Mercury (556–570), who ironically tells him that he ought not be sleeping so calmly since danger lies ahead. The solemnity of a sacrifice is marked by spondees in *Aeneid 2,*

> *sollemnis taurum ingentem mactabat ad aras* (202),

a line whose ponderous rhythm may also suggest the size of the bull. Similarly, the slow, lumbering movement and hideous bulk of the Cyclops are famously represented by the rhythm of this elision-filled, spondaic line:

> *monstrum horrendum informe ingens qui lumen ademptum* (*A.* 3.658).

---

[33] It is also somewhat unusual to place a noun next to a qualifying adjective that is metrically equivalent. Here again, the lack of variation may suggest lethargy and sleep, cf. *molles somnos* (*G.* 3.435) and *somni pingues* (*Am.* 1.13.7) with McKeown's note.

[34] Cf. *A.* 2.9.

[35] Cf. *A.* 3.466–468, three consecutive spondaic lines, whose rhythm may suggest the magnificence of Helenus's gifts to Aeneas.

The pointed juxtaposition of dactyls and spondees in the same line can be as metrically effective as lines of uniform rhythm:

saxa per et scopulos et depressas conualles (*G.* 3.276).

Here, the unusual postponement of the preposition *per* eliminates the spondaic opening of *per saxa et scopulos* and gives the line a dactylic rhythm to imitate the excited gallop of mares in love, while the spondaic line-ending may suggest, by contrast, "a smooth, even gallop along the level valleys" (Page), "eventual weariness" (Williams), or, conversely, nothing in particular (Thomas). Even the introduction of a single, strategically-placed spondee, coupled with the absence of a strong caesura, in Horace's

labitur et labetur in omne uolubilis aeuum (*Ep.* 1.2.43)

can suggest the ebb and flow of a river's current.[36]

Sometimes the interaction of rhythm and words can be more subtly and intricately developed than a simple onomatopoetic correspondence of sound to meaning. When discussing meter in his *Ars Poetica*, Horace notes that "not just any judge can spot unmetrical poetry," in a line that violates several rules of the Latin hexameter:

non quiuis uidet immodulata poemata iudex (263).

Notice the absence of a penthemimeral caesura, partly the result of the placement of "*uidet*," which causes a diaeresis at the end of the second foot, itself a violation. Lacking a strong third foot caesura, Horace ought to have one in the fourth foot, but the break is a weak one. Thus, the line's rhythm ironically serves as an example of the poorly modulated verse that foolish judges fail to recognize.[37] At the same time, however, the line is paradoxically praiseworthy, for its irregular rhythm serves a meaningful purpose that a "good" judge can spot.

[36] Ezra Pound praised Homer for a similar technique in the line, παρὰ θῖνα πολυφλοίσβοιο θαλάσσης, describing the "rush of the waves on the sea-beach and their recession" (*Literary Essays* 250).

[37] Since weak caesurae are quite customary in Greek poetry, and since it is precisely at this point in his poem that Horace stresses the importance of studying the "*exemplaria Graeca*" (*AP* 268), it is perhaps not far-fetched to detect further irony in the line.

EXERCISE IX: RHYTHMIC EFFECTS

Translate and scan the following lines. Then speculate on the connection between rhythm and meaning.

1.   nautae
   adnixi torquent spumas et caerula uerrunt.
2. fertur equis auriga neque audit currus habenas.
3. urunt Lethaeo perfusa papauera somno.
4. exstinctum Nymphae crudeli funere Daphnin flebant.
5. illi inter sese multa ui bracchia tollunt.
6. labitur uncta carina uolat super impetus undas.
7. inuadunt urbem somno uinoque sepultam.
8. constitit atque oculis Phrygia agmina circumspexit.
9. haec ubi dicta dedit, lacrimantem et multa uolentem
   dicere deseruit, tenuisque recessit in auras.
10. intenti exspectant signum, exsultantiaque haurit
    corda pauor pulsans, laudumque arrecta cupido.
    inde ubi clara dedit sonitum tuba, finibus omnes,
    haud mora, prosiluere suis; ferit aethera clamor.
11. saepe etiam immensum caelo uenit agmen aquarum
    et foedam glomerant tempestatem imbribus atris
    collectae ex alto nubes; ruit arduus aether
    et pluuia ingenti sata laeta boumque labores
    diluit.
12. hoc dicens ferrum aduerso sub pectore condit
    feruidus. ast illi soluuntur frigore membra
    uitaque cum gemitu fugit indignata sub umbras.

PART B: CONSONANTS AND VOWELS

Assonance (the repetition of vowel sounds), consonance (the repetition of consonant sounds), and alliteration (the repetition of initial sounds) can be used for a
variety of purposes ranging from onomatopoeia to more subtly suggestive sound
effects (e.g., the establishment of a mood) to artistic patterns of arrangement lending emphasis or variety to a given passage. Ancient commentators held that certain letters had particular intrinsic qualities (e.g., *l* is sweet, *r* and *z* are rough and
noble, and *s* is unattractive, while *m* and *n* sound like a horn[38]), but the poets' actual
practices suggest a more fluid use of sound patterns that are perhaps best under-
stood in the context of specific lines.

The repetition of *s* sounds, for instance, may suggest the hissing of snakes,

> *saucius at serpens sinuosa uolumina uersat*
>
> *arrectisque horret squamis et sibilat ore*
>
> *arduus insurgens* (*A.* 11.753–5),

or the hiss of anger in Dido's rebuke of Aeneas,

> *dissimulare etiam sperasti, perfide, tantum*
>
> *posse nefas tacitusque mea decedere terra?* (*A.* 4.305–6),[39]

or the splash of water,

> *inter saxa uirum spumosa immerserat unda* (*A.* 6.174).

Conversely, *s* can convey the calm of sleep:

---

[38] Dion. Hal. *De Comp.* 14 writes that λ "falls pleasurably on the ear"; ρ and ζ are rough
and therefore convey an austere nobility; "σ is an unattractive, disagreeable letter, very
offensive when used in excess" and "more suited to a brute beast than a rational being"; long
vowels are more powerful and produce a more attractive sound than short vowels, none of
which is beautiful, but ο is "less ugly" than ε. Demetrius *On Style* 174–175 praises the
beauty of λ and ν and notes that vowels are generally smooth and consonants rough. The
Romans often called *r* the *littera canina*.

[39] Cf. Eur. *Med.* ἔσωσά σ', ὡς ἴσασιν Ἑλλήνων ὅσοι . . ., with Page's note *ad loc.*

post ubi iam thalamis se composuere, siletur

in noctem, fessosque sopor suus occupat artus (*G.* 4.189), and

saepe leui somnum suadebit inire susurro (*E.* 1.55).

Repeated *t*'s may echo the thundering of a storm,

tempestas sine more furit tonitruque tremescunt

ardua terrarum et campi; ruit aethere toto

turbidus imber aqua (*A.* 5.694–696),

while the repetition of *c* is suggestive of Dido's torment as she is plucked apart by love; notice also how repeated *u*'s are added to convey the queen's pain and grief:

uulnus alit uenis et caeco carpitur igni.

multa uiri uirtus animo multusque recursat

gentis honos (*A.* 4.2–4).

V's have a similar mournful effect in,

continuo auditae uoces uagitus et ingens (*A.* 6.426)

and

hinc exaudiri uoces et uerba uocantis

uisa uiri (*A.* 4.460–1),

in which the *u*'s also convey the eerie atmosphere of the scene, as Dido imagines she hears Sychaeus calling out to her. *M* will often suggest the rumbling murmur of the sea,

interea magno misceri murmure pontum (*A.* 1.124),

but it can just as easily evoke the sleepy softness of shaded grass, especially when combined with *n*:

muscosi fontes et somno mollior herba (*E.* 7.45).

The softness of *m* can also have the negative connotations of eastern decadence and effeminacy:

> *et nunc ille Paris cum semiuiro comitatu,*
>
> *Maeonia mentum mitra crinemque madentem*
>
> *subnexus, rapto potitur* (A. 4.215–17).

The scornful tone of these lines is reinforced by the subsequent alliteration of *f*, which Cicero considered an unpleasant letter.[40]

> *nos munera templis*
>
> *quippe tuis ferimus, famamque fovemus inanem* (217–218).

In *Aeneid* 6, snarling *r*'s convey the harsh suffering that the souls judged by Minos would willingly endure on earth if they could only escape the misery of the underworld:

> *quam uellent aethere in alto*
>
> *nunc et pauperiem et duros perferre labores* (436–437).

To this list, many more and different examples could be added, and readers are encouraged to observe and assess the significance of whatever repetitions they find.

It must be stressed, however, that it is neither necessary nor advisable for a poet to reserve alliteration for attention-getting passages in which a single letter is repeated five or six times and the onomatopoetic effects are obvious. More subtle repetitions can greatly enhance the character of a line or a passage. Consider, for instance, the Aeolus episode of *Aeneid* 1. Aeolus, king of the winds, is persuaded by Juno to stir up a storm, and throughout the passage repeated letters reflect the sounds of the rising tempest. The winds, eager to break out of their restraints, rumble spondaically with the sound of *m*'s, only to be checked by the harsh force of *c*'s:

> *illi indignantes magno cum murmure montis*
>
> *circum claustra fremunt* (55–56).

Aeolus is ordered to strike force into the winds with the powerful alliteration of consonantal *u*:

---

[40] *Orator* 163; cf. Quintilian *Inst.* 12.10.

incute uim uentis summersasque obrue puppis (69).[41]

When the god strikes the mountain with his spear-shaft, the cracking sound is marked by alliterative *c*'s:

haec ubi dicta, cauum conuersa cuspide montem
impulit in latus (81–2),

while consonantal *u*'s record the sweeping sound of rushing winds in

. . . *ac uenti uelut agmine facto* (82), and
Africus et uastos uoluunt ad litora fluctus (85).

Notice that in each instance a letter may recur only two or three times, and some readers may therefore be inclined to discount their significance, but excessive alliteration can be clumsily obvious and should be used sparingly. Cicero famously advised that "we shall avoid the excessive recurrence of the same letter," citing as a negative example Ennius's notorious, "O Tite, tute, Tati, tibi tanta, tyranne, tulisti" (*ad Her.* 4.17). To an Augustan aesthetic as well, subtlety is the greater virtue.

---

[41] Winbolt 157 notes Lucretius's fondness for using *u* to convey force.

EXERCISE X: ALLITERATION, ETC.

Translate the following passages and identify all instances of alliteration, consonance, and assonance. Then suggest the significance of the repetitions you find. Any complementary rhythmic effects should also be noted.

1. et molem mirantur equi . . .
2. tum Zephyri posuere, premit placida aequora pontus.
3. insontem infando indicio, quia bella uetabat,
   demisere neci, nunc cassum lumine lugent.
4. [Aeneas sees a vision of Hector . . .] aterque cruento
   puluere, perque pedes traiectus lora tumentis.
5. pectora quorum inter fluctus arrecta iubaeque
   sanguineae superant undas; pars cetera pontum
   pone legit, sinuatque immensa uolumine terga.
   fit sonitus spumante salo; iamque arua tenebant,
   ardentisque oculos suffecti sanguine et igni,
   sibila lambebant linguis uibrantibus ora.
6. mens agitat molem et magno se corpore miscet.
7. ne, pueri, ne tanta animis adsuescite bella,
   neu patriae ualidas in uiscera uertite uires.
8. continuo uentis surgentibus aut freta ponti
   incipiunt agitata tumescere et aridus altis
   montibus audiri fragor aut resonantia longe
   litora misceri et nemorum increbrescere murmur.
9. nec rapit inmensos orbis per humum neque tanto
   squameus in spiram tractu se colligit anguis.
10. stabant orantes primi transmittere cursum
    tendebantque manus ripae ulterioris amore.

PART C: WORD ORDER

Like the use of vowel and consonant patterns, the arrangement of words within a line can reinforce the sense of a passage. In Vergil's first *Georgic*, for instance, the poet advises against planting seeds, "the hope of the year," before the earth is ready to receive them:

> *inuitae properes anni spem credere terrae* (224).

Observe how the seeds, represented by the words *anni spem*, are metaphorically "planted" within the *inuitae . . . terrae*. Similarly, in *Aeneid* 9, a terrified Rhoetus tries to escape from Euryalus by hiding behind a huge krater:

> *sed magnum metuens se post cratera tegebat* (346).

Here, little Rhoetus (*se*) is sheltered by the *magnum . . . cratera* which surrounds him.[42]

Sometimes words are placed next to each other for dramatic contrast. When Vergil first mentions Carthage in *Aeneid* 1, he writes,

> *Vrbs antiqua fuit (Tyrii tenuere coloni)*
> *Karthago, Italiam contra Tiberinaque longe*
> *ostia* (12–14).

Note that the poet could have written *Karthago contra Italiam* – a more natural word order with more logical caesurae – but instead he daringly postpones the preposition to juxtapose Carthage and Italy, and thereby underscore a central conflict of the poem and of Roman history. Conversely, a neighboring adjective and noun may be *attracted* to one another even though they do not agree grammatically. In Vergil's

> *siluestrem tenui musam meditaris auena* (*E*. 1.2),

---

[42] The principle of "The Pictoral Arrangement of Words in Vergil" was first demonstrated, along with these examples, by Arthur Milton Young at the APA's sixty-fifth annual meeting, *TAPA* 64 (1933): li–lii. See also D. Lateiner, "Mimetic Syntax: Metaphor from Word Order, Especially in Ovid," *AJPh* 111 (1990): 204–237.

the words *tenui* and *musam*, although not in grammatical agreement, combine to form the "slender muse" indicative of the refined poetic style advocated by the poet Callimachus and paraphrased by Vergil himself in *Eclogue* 6.4–5.

Enjambment (a "striding-over," in which the sense of one line is completed by a word at the start of the next) is often used to "express sudden and violent action,"[43] especially when the enjambed word is a dactyl. A spear speeding through the air suddenly reaches its target in the lines

> *illa uolans umeri surgunt qua tegmina summa*
> *incidit* (*A*. 10.476–477).

In *Aeneid* 5, Vergil similarly defers his verb when massive Entellus abruptly falls to the ground:

> *ipse grauis grauiterque ad terram pondere uasto*
> *concidit* (447–478).

And in the first *Georgic*, the postponement of *deicit* emphasizes the force of Jupiter's thunderbolts:

> *ille flagranti*
> *aut Atho aut Rhodopen aut alta Ceraunia telo*
> *deicit* (131–133).

The enjambment of an adjective can be effective as well. When Venus pleads with Jupiter at the council of the gods in *Aeneid* 10, her contempt for Juno's relentless hounding of the Trojans is emphasized by the emphatic positioning of *dura* at the start of the second line:

> *si nulla est regio Teucris quam det tua coniunx*
> *dura* . . . (44–45).

The use of enjambment, like the practice of beginning a new sentence in the sixth foot, also serves a stylistic purpose: to avoid the rhythmic monotony of the frequent coincidence of line and sentence endings.

Other patterns of arrangement function on a more subtle level. A so-called "golden line" consists of "two substantives and two adjectives, with a verb

---

[43] J. Marouzeau, *L'ordre des mots en latin* (Paris, 1953) 307.

betwixt them to keep the peace" (Dryden).[44] Strictly speaking a true golden line follows the pattern, Adjective A – Adjective B – Verb – Noun A – Noun B, e.g.,

>   *mollia luteola pingit uaccinia calta (E. 2.50).*

Note, however, that the Romans had no such term as *uersus aureus*. Slight variations are equally noteworthy, and the effect is not significantly diminished either by the insertion of a preposition,

>   *mitis in apricis coquitur uindemia saxis (G. 2.522),*

or by the slight displacement of the verb,

>   *et curuae rigidum falces conflantur in ensem (G. 1.508).*

Alternatively, a line can be arranged as a chiasmus, in which the nouns and adjectives crisscross, with one pair inside the other and the verb in the middle (i.e. Adjective A – Adjective B – Verb – Noun B – Noun A):

>   *unde cauae tepido sudant umore lacunae (G. 1.117).*

Chiastic arrangement of nouns and adjectives can also occur without a verb in between:

>   *uicinae ruptis inter se legibus urbes*
>   *arma ferunt (G. 1.510–511).*

---

[44] Preface to the *Silvae*, 1685. It is often forgotten that Dryden introduces his famous phrase in order to criticize Claudian for his excessive use of "golden lines." Dryden's terse and unabashedly opinionated judgments about the metrical style of several Latin hexameter poets are interesting enough to quote at length: "All the versification and little variety of Claudian is included within the compass of four or five lines, and then he begins again in the same tenor; perpetually closing his sense at the end of a verse, and that verse commonly that which they call golden, or two substantives and two adjectives, with a verb betwixt them to keep the peace. Ovid, with all his sweetness, has as little variety of numbers and sound as he; he is always, as it were, upon the hand-gallop, and his verse runs upon carpet-ground. He avoids, like the other, all synalephas, or cutting off one vowel when it comes before another in the following word; so that, minding only smoothness, he wants both variety and majesty. But to return to Virgil: tho' he is smooth where smoothness is requir'd, yet he is so far from affecting it, that he seems rather to disdain it; frequently he makes use of synalephas, and concludes his sense in the middle of his verse. He is everywhere above the conceits of epigrammatic wit, and gross hyperboles; he maintains majesty in the midst of plainness; he shines, but glares not; and is stately without ambition, which is the vice of Lucan."

Such elegantly balanced lines are often used to lend a dignified tone to a passage. At the start of the fourth *Eclogue*, a chiasmus conveys a sense of prophetic grandeur:

> *ultima Cumaei uenit iam carminis aetas* (4).

Similarly, when Aeneas establishes athletic contests in honor of the anniversary of his father's death, the solemnity of the occasion is emphasized by an elaborately patterned line:

> *prima citae Teucris ponam certamina classis* (5.66).

Sometimes a golden line will add gravity and emotional power to a passage. When discussing the assassination of Julius Caesar, Vergil uses a such a line to describe how the sun covered its shining head, frightening a godless age:

> *impiaque aeternam timuerunt saecula noctem* (*G*. 1.468).

Symmetrical patterns are also used to mark the end of a passage. In *Georgics* 2, for instance, Vergil concludes his discussion of the life "golden Saturn" lived with a golden line:

> *impositos duris crepitare incudibus ensis* (540).

The structural balance of such lines provides a sense of formal closure in much the same way that rhymed couplets effectively end scenes and major speeches in Shakespeare.

Equilibrium of another sort can be achieved through verbal repetition, often adding emphasis to a point or setting up opposition or connection.[45] When Aeneas declares,

> *socer arma Latinus habeto,*
> *imperium sollemne socer . . .* (192–193),

he uses the chiastic repetition of *socer* to stress that his alliance with Latinus will be secured through marriage to Lavinia. Similarly, the repetition of *pariter* in *Aeneid*

---

[45] The definitive work on this subject is Jeffrey Wills's magnificent *Repetition in Latin Poetry* (Oxford, 1996).

8 underscores the equal cooperation of the Trojan and Arcadian allies as they make joint sacrifice:

> *mactat lectas de more bidentis*
> *Euandrus pariter, pariter Troiana iuuentus* (544–545).

But verbal repetition is not always so serious, especially in the hands of Ovid, who often arranges multiple repeated words into an elaborate chiasmus. He famously declares that women come to the theater to see and be seen,

> *spectatum ueniunt, ueniunt spectentur ut ipsae* (*AA* 1.99)

and, even more playfully, that he will easily fall for both blondes and brunettes:

> *candida me capiet, capiet me flaua puella* (*Am.* 2.4.39).

Vergil also uses repetition in an amatory context, and in *Eclogue* 10 he sets up an elegantly elliptical comparison:

> *malle pati tenerisque meos incidere amores*
> *arboribus: crescent illae, crescetis, amores* (53–54).

The poet will carve the name of his beloved into young trees, and just as those trees will grow, so the carvings will grow, so his love will grow, and so her fame will grow.[46]

It is a hallmark of the Vergilian style to fuse rhythm, diction, sound, and sense into a harmonious unit, even on the smallest textual level. In a deservedly famous passage from *Aeneid* 4, Dido and Aeneas take shelter in a cave when a rainstorm interrupts their hunt. Vergil describes the moment this way:

> *speluncam Dido dux et Troianus eandem*
> *deueniunt* (165–166).

---

[46] The sense is nicely, if only partially, captured by Spenser:

> Her name in every tree I will endosse,
> That as the trees do grow, her name may grow:
> And in the ground each where will it engrosse,
> And fill with stones, that all men may it know.
> (*Colin Clouts Come Home Againe* 632–635)

The placement of every word is significant to the scene: "Dido" and the "dux Troianus" are literally surrounded by "same cave" (*speluncam . . . eandem*). In addition, the postponement of *et* (necessary to avoid hiatus at the caesura) produces the strongly alliterative *Dido dux*, and the resulting word order attracts the term "dux" to the queen[47] even as it remains a noun for *Troianus* to modify. This double syntax perhaps underscores the thematically significant, and ultimately tragic, point that Dido and Aeneas could have formed a mighty alliance had fate allowed it. Alternatively, the tangled word order of "Dido dux et Troianus" may suggest the lovers' embrace within the cave. Finally, the enjambment of the dactylic *deueniunt* following a spondaic line conveys the suddenness with which Dido and Aeneas are driven to the cave. Most of us will never achieve this level of sophistication, but it is a worthy goal.

---

[47] Cf. 1.364, *dux femina facti.*

EXERCISE XI: WORD ORDER

Translate the following lines and note how the words are arranged. Then explain any connection between word order and meaning. As always, any complementary effects of rhythm and sound should also be identified. Pay particular attention to the final passage, which contains an impressively broad array of poetic devices.

1. aureus et foliis et lento uimine ramus.

2.   (turris) ea lapsa repente ruinam
cum sonitu trahit et Danaum super agmina late
incidit.

3.   ... etiam Parnasia laurus
parua sub ingenti matris se subicit umbra.

4. grandiaque effossis mirabitur ossa sepulchris.

5. bis Tusci Rutulos egere ad moenia uersos.

6. magnaque cum magno ueniet tritura calore.

7.   ... "cessas in uota precesque,
Tros" ait "Aenea? cessas? neque enim ante dehiscent
attonitae magna ora domus." et talia fata
conticuit. gelidus Teucris per dura cucurrit
ossa tremor.

8. in segetem ueluti cum flamma furentibus Austris
incidit, aut rapidus montano flumine torrens
sternit agros, sternit sata laeta boumque labores.

9. iam grauis aequabat luctus et mutua Mauors
funera; caedebant pariter pariterque ruebant
uictores uictique, neque his fuga nota neque illis.

10. sic fatus, ualidis ingentem uiribus hastam
in latus inque feri curuam compagibus aluum
contorsit: stetit illa tremens, uteroque recusso
insonuere cauae gemitumque dedere cauernae.

EXERCISE XII: SOUND AND SENSE
IN *ECLOGUE* 6

Read an *Eclogue* and identify and discuss any unusual rhythms and sound effects. *Eclogue* 6 is printed below, but the exercise may be profitably repeated with any or all of the remaining nine. Remember, there is no better way to learn about Latin meter than by reading Latin poetry.

Prima Syracosio dignata est ludere uersu,
nostra nec erubuit siluas habitare Thalia.
cum canerem reges et proelia, Cynthius aurem
uellit, et admonuit: 'pastorem, Tityre, pinguis
pascere oportet ouis, deductum dicere carmen.'
nunc ego (namque super tibi erunt, qui dicere laudes,
Vare, tuas cupiant, et tristia condere bella)
agrestem tenui meditabor harundine Musam.
non iniussa cano: si quis tamen haec quoque, si quis
captus amore leget, te nostrae, Vare, myricae,
te nemus omne canet; nec Phoebo gratior ulla est,
quam sibi quae Vari praescripsit pagina nomen.
        Pergite, Pierides! Chromis et Mnasyllos in antro
Silenum pueri somno uidere iacentem,
inflatum hesterno uenas, ut semper, Iaccho:
serta procul tantum capiti delapsa iacebant,
et grauis attrita pendebat cantharus ansa.
adgressi (nam saepe senex spe carminis ambo
luserat) iniciunt ipsis ex uincula sertis:
addit se sociam, timidisque superuenit Aegle,
Aegle, Naiadum pulcherrima, iamque uidenti
sanguineis frontem moris et tempora pingit.
ille dolum ridens, 'quo uincula nectitis?' inquit.
'soluite me, pueri; satis est potuisse uideri:
carmina, quae uoltis, cognoscite; carmina uobis,
huic aliud mercedis erit.' simul incipit ipse.
tum uero in numerum Faunosque ferasque uideres
ludere, tum rigidas motare cacumina quercus;

nec tantum Phoebo gaudet Parnasia rupes,
nec tantum Rhodope miratur et Ismarus Orphea.
    namque canebat, uti magnum per inane coacta
semina terrarumque animaeque marisque fuissent,
et liquidi simul ignis; ut his exordia primis
omnia et ipse tener mundi concreuerit orbis;
tum durare solum et discludere Nerea ponto
coeperit, et rerum paulatim sumere formas;
iamque nouum terrae stupeant lucescere solem,
altius atque cadant submotis nubibus imbres;
incipiant siluae cum primum surgere, cumque
rara per ignaros errent animalia montis.
hinc lapides Pyrrhae iactos, Saturnia regna,
Caucasiasque refert uolucres, furtumque Promethei:
his adiungit, Hylan nautae quo fonte relictum
clamassent, ut litus 'Hyla, Hyla!' omne sonaret.
et fortunatam, si numquam armenta fuissent,
Pasiphaen niuei solatur amore iuuenci.
a, uirgo infelix, quae te dementia cepit!
Proetides inplerunt falsis mugitibus agros:
at non tam turpis pecudum tamen ulla secuta est
concubitus, quamuis collo timuisset aratrum,
et saepe in leui quaesisset cornua fronte.
a, uirgo infelix, tu nunc in montibus erras:
ille, latus niueum molli fultus hyacintho,
ilice sub nigra pallentis ruminat herbas,
aut aliquam in magno sequitur grege. 'claudite, nymphae,
Dictaeae nymphae, nemorum iam claudite saltus,
si qua forte ferant oculis sese obuia nostris
errabunda bouis uestigia; forsitan illum,
aut herba captum uiridi, aut armenta secutum,
perducant aliquae stabula ad Gortynia uaccae.
tum canit Hesperidum miratam mala puellam;
tum Phaethontiadas musco circumdat amaro
corticis, atque solo proceras erigit alnos.
tum canit, errantem Permessi ad flumina Gallum
Aonas in montis ut duxerit una sororum,
utque uiro Phoebi chorus adsurrexerit omnis;
ut Linus haec illi, diuino carmine pastor,
floribus atque apio crinis ornatus amaro,

dixerit: 'hos tibi dant calamos, en accipe, Musae,
Ascraeo quos ante seni, quibus ille solebat
cantando rigidas deducere montibus ornos:
his tibi Grynei nemoris dicatur origo,
ne quis sit lucus, quo se plus iactet Apollo.'
quid loquar aut Scyllam Nisi, quam fama secuta est
candida succinctam latrantibus inguina monstris
Dulichias uexasse rates, et gurgite in alto,
a, timidos nautas canibus lacerasse marinis,
aut ut mutatos Terei narrauerit artus;
quas illi Philomela dapes, quae dona pararit,
quo cursu deserta petiuerit, et quibus ante
infelix sua tecta superuolitauerit alis?
omnia, quae Phoebo quondam meditante, beatus
audiit Eurotas, iussitque ediscere laurus,
ille canit: pulsae referunt ad sidera ualles;
cogere donec ouis stabulis numerumque referri
iussit, et inuito processit Vesper Olympo.

EXERCISE XIII: HEXAMETER JUMBLES I

In the exercise below, each group of long and short marks separated by the symbol | represents a word. Rearrange each set so it scans as a proper hexameter line, including a main caesura. You may find it helpful to copy each "word" onto a separate index card and then try to rearrange the cards on a table.

1. ∪–|–∪|–∪|––|∪––|∪∪––
2. –|∪–|–∪|∪–∪|∪∪–|–∪∪–∪
3. ∪–|–∪|∪∪–|––|∪––|∪∪–∪
4. ∪∪|–∪|∪∪–|∪∪–|∪––|–∪∪–
5. ∪|–∪|––|–∪∪|–––|∪–∪∪
6. ––|∪∪–|–∪∪|–––|–∪∪–
7. –|∪∪–|––|––|–∪∪ |––∪∪
8. ∪–|–∪|––|∪–∪|∪∪– |––∪
9. ∪∪–|––|–∪∪|–∪∪–|––∪∪
10. –|∪–|––|∪–∪|––∪|∪∪–∪
11. ∪∪|–|––|––|–∪∪–|––∪∪
12. ∪∪–|––|∪––|––∪|–––
13. ∪∪|–|–|∪–|–∪|––|––|–∪∪
14. ∪∪|–|–|–|–∪|––|–∪∪|–∪∪
15. ∪∪|–|–∪|∪––|–∪∪–|–––
16. –|–∪|∪∪–|–∪∪|∪––|–∪∪–
17. ∪–|–∪|–∪∪|––|∪––|––∪
18. –|–|–|–∪|–∪∪|––|–––
19. –|∪–|–∪|–∪|∪∪–|–∪∪|– –
20. –|–|–|∪–|–∪|–∪|–∪∪|––
21. –|–|∪∪–|∪∪–|–∪∪|––|––
22. ∪|∪–|–∪|∪–∪|––∪|–––∪
23. ∪∪|––|––|––|–∪∪|–∪∪–
24. ∪|–|–∪|–∪|∪–|∪∪–|∪–∪|––
25. –|–|–∪|∪∪–|∪∪–|––|∪––

48

EXERCISE XIV: HEXAMETER JUMBLES II

In this exercise, all long and short syllables are marked for you, but some final syllables may be lengthened or elided depending upon their position with respect to other words. Following the rules of prosody and meter you have learned, rearrange the following lines to form proper hexameters. Again, you may find it helpful to write the words on index cards and experiment with various arrangements.

1. rūpērūnt mēssēs īmmēnsāē īllĭŭs hōrrĕă
2. ădōrĕt āgrēstĭs Cĕrĕrĕm cūnctă pūbēs tĭbī
3. dīctīs ēxārsĭt tālĭbŭs Tūrnī uĭŏlēntĭă
4. īgnĕŭs cāērŭlĕŭs Ēurōs plŭuĭăm dēnūntĭăt
5. hīnc Ēuphrātēs bēllŭm mŏuĕt īllīnc Gērmānĭă
6. ārbŏrĭbŭs crĕāndīs ēst nātŭă prīncĭpĭō uărĭă
7. ātquĕ īmpōnĕrĕ īnsĕrĕrĕ mŏdŭs nĕc ŏcŭlōs sĭmplēx
8. uērō tērrāē pōssūnt ōmnĭă ōmnēs nĕc fērrĕ
9. ārbōs făcĭēmquĕ lāūrō īngēns īpsă sĭmīllĭmă
10. ādsĭdŭŭm āēstās ălĭēnīs ātquĕ hīc mēnsĭbŭs uēr
11. bĭs bĭs ārbōs grăuĭdāē pĕcŭdēs pōmīs ūtĭlĭs
12. ādlŭĭt ăn īnfrā mărĕ mĕmŏrĕm quŏd quŏdquĕ sūprā
13. ăpĭbŭs căsĭās hŭmĭlĭs mĭnīstrăt rōrēmquĕ vīx
14. dīmēnsă nŭmĕrīs ōmnĭă părĭbŭs sīnt uĭārŭm
15. ĕt fāstīgĭă fŏsĭtăn quāē quāē rās scrŏbĭbŭs sīnt
16. āūsĭm cōmmīttĕrĕ sūlcō tĕnŭī uĕl uītĕm
17. sŭpĕrăt ŏlĕāstĕr īnfēlīx fŏlĭīs ămārīs
18. ĕt hōc nūtrītŏr ŏlīuăm Pācī pīnguĕm plăcĭtăm
19. āēquē Bācchēĭă dōnă mĕmŏrāndŭm quĭd tŭlērūnt
20. ălĭŭs āūrō cōndĭt dēfēssōquĕ īncŭbăt ŏpēs
21. ăd ĭtĕr Lătīnōs mūrōsquĕ nōbīs nūnc rēgĕm
22. crūdēlĕ fūnŭs īnfēlīx nātī uĭdēbĭs
23. āddĭt ĕquōs ĕt hōstĕm quĭbŭs spŏlĭăuĕrăt tēlă
24. cāēlō dīmōuĕrăt gĕlĭdăm lūx tērtĭă ūmbrăm
25. crĕpĭtāns grāndō hōrrĭdă ĭn mūltă sălĭt tăm tēctīs

EXERCISE XV: HEXAMETER JUMBLES III

In this exercise you will need to determine the vowel quantities for yourself. Once that has been accomplished, the task is identical to that of the previous exercise. Rearrange the following sentences to form proper hexameter lines. There are no elisions. In some cases, more than one solution is possible.

1. digna omnia tuis ingentibus coeptis sponde
2. nulla gloria sine te meis rebus quaeretur
3. equos audit, signa sequentum et strepitus audit
4. Turnus subridens pectore sedato olli
5. Troes uersi formidine trepida diffugiunt
6. et Mnestheus inquit: "quo tenditis, quo deinde fugam"
7. ait haec et medius in densos hostis prorumpit
8. nam Thymbre tibi Euandrius caput ensis abstulit
9. flammas ouantis sedens ille uictor despectat
10. genitor fata canens Halaesum siluis celarat
11. aequis ducibusque et uiribus concurrant agmina
12. fata sua mox illos sub maiore hoste manent
13. sanguis frigidus in praecordia Arcadibus coit
14. genitor natum dictis amicis tum adfatur
15. num mage telum penetrabile nostrum sit aspice
16. frustra ille telum calidum de uulnere rapit
17. inde procul hastam infensam Mago contenderat
18. hoc manes Anchisae patris, hoc Iulus sensit
19. moribundus excussus aruis curru uoluitur
20. pius Aeneas amaris dictis quem adfatur
21. tum mucrone pectus animae latebras recludit
22. interea Iuppiter Iunonem ultro compellat
23. pereat Teucrisque nunc sanguine pio poenas det
24. rex Olympi aetherii cui sic breuiter fatur
25. sic Mezentius alacer in hostis densos ruit

EXERCISE XVI: HEXAMETER
JUMBLES IV, ELISIONS

Rearrange the following lines to form proper hexameters. There is at least one elision in each line. In some cases, more than one solution is possible.

1. et moriens cruento ore hostilem terram petit
2. te limite lato ducam et haec uasta ego dabo
3. tellus gemitum dat et super clipeum ingens intonat
4. quae moenia ultra quos iam muros alios habetis?
5. non mare non nubila non ipsi inter se cedit
6. omnia obnixa contra stant pugna anceps diu
7. sequuntur una uia sanguis eademque animusque
8. sic ille ore placido haec auditis reddidit
9. inter media milia Tisiphone pallida saeuit
10. ipse per omnes mortis animam sontem dedissem
11. Aenean ter uoce magna hic uocauit atque
12. obuius hasta infesta et effatus tantum subit
13. nec ulli diuum parcimus nec mortem horremus
14. oro si qua uenia uictis hostibus est per hoc unum
15. stramine agresti hic ponunt iuuenem sublimem
16. huic morti opponere se Turnum aequis fuerat
17. ciuibus miseris ignem nunc supponite et ite
18. haec dixerat unoque ore omnes fremebant eadem
19. at oro tu succurre relictae et inopem solare
20. ne ne uero me impellite ad pugnas tales
21. fessis rebus succurrite et in medium consulite
22. mihi licet arma mortemque minetur, equidem dicam
23. ad tua magna et te pater consulta reuertor nunc
24. o si uirtutis quicquam quamquam solitae adesset
25. certatim ipse Turnus furens in proelia cingitur

BONUS: Rearrange to form a hexameter and explain what is unusual about the line that you get:

Noemonaque Alcandrumque Prytanimque Haliumque

EXERCISE XVII: HEXAMETER JUMBLES V, MIXED LINES

Rearrange the following lines to form proper hexameters. Some lines contain one or more elisions, but others contain none. Weak caesurae are also present in some lines. More than one solution is often possible.

1. at inermem dextram Aeneas pius tendebat
2. interea Olympi omnipotentis domus panditur
3. et parant flammis torrere et saxo frangere
4. o Calliope precor uos canenti adspirate
5. ductori Turno furenti in parte diuersa
6. formidine trepida uersi Troes diffugiunt
7. agmina fuga bis confusa per muros uertit
8. at uiribus magnis Pallas hastam emittit
9. sic uictor Aeneas in toto aequore desaeuit
10. Acron de finibus antiquis Corythi uenerat
11. secuti paeana laetum socii conclamant
12. quae Acherontis fert hinc uia ad undas Tartarei
13. hic turbidus gurges caeno uoragine uastaque
14. eructat atque aestuat omnem harenam Cocyto
15. horrendus portitor seruat flumina et has aquas
16. Charon cui terribili squalore mento plurima
17. lumina flamma stant canities inculta iacet
18. sordidus amictus ex umeris dependet nodo
19. ipse ministrat subigit ratem conto uelisque
20. cymba et ferruginea corpora subuectat
21. sed iam senectus senior deo uiridisque cruda
22. ruebat huc effusa omnis turba ad ripas
23. atque matres corpora uita defunctaque uiri
24. innuptaeque puellae pueri magnanimum heroum
25. rogis iuuenes impositique ante parentum ora

EXERCISE XVIII: HEXAMETER JUMBLES VI, DOUBLE LINES

When each of the following sentences is arranged properly, it will form two hexameter lines. The line division is given in sentences 1–3 but not in 4–10. Elisions may occur, and more than one solution is often possible.

1. quin etiam bis medios hostes tum inuaserat
   bis fuga uertit agmina confusa per muros
2. instant interea Rutuli circum omnibus portis
   cingere moenia flammis et sternere uiros caede
3. Saturnia uix funem rumpit proram attigerat,
   auulsamque nauem per aequora reuoluta rapit
4. Turnus dubius haud aliter improperata uestigia retro refert et mens
   ira exaestuat
5. quianam sententia uersa retro, tantumque animis iniquis certatis,
   magni caelicolae?
6. contulerant illi certamina duri belli inter sese: Aeneas media nocte
   freta secabat
7. ter denis nauibus tot proceres lecti Troiae subsidio ibant et secabant
   campos salis aere
8. Alcides iuuenem audiit magnumque gemitum imo sub corde premit
   lacrimasque inanes effundit
9. ter utramque uiam conatus, ter Iuno maxima continuit iuuenemque
   repressit miserata animi
10. infelix uulnere alieno sternitur, caelumque aspicit et moriens Argos
    dulces reminiscitur

EXERCISE XIX: THE END OF THE LINE I

Translate the following phrases into Latin that will scan as the last two feet of a hexameter line: $-\cup\cup\ |\ \cup\ \bar{\cup}$. The following models will apply:

1–10	$-\cup\cup\ \vdots\ -\bar{\cup}$	sidera noctis
11–20	$-\cup\ \vdots\ \cup-\bar{\cup}$	dona puellae

1.	extending (her) arms	bracchium tendo
2.	the armaments of Caesar	arma Caesar
3.	to walk softly	leniter eo
4.	open the lock	claustrum relaxo
5.	she knew songs	carmen nosco
6.	I saw stars	sidus uideo
7.	the cold of night	frigus (pl.) noctis
8.	the troops of Rhesus	agmen Rhesus
9.	he perceived the chains	vinculum sentio
10.	she demands rewards	praemium posco
11.	Minerva's arms	arma Minerua
12.	greater than Homer	magnus Homerus
13.	you (s.) will often ask	saepe rogo
14.	send the girl	puella mitto
15.	the image of death	imago mors
16.	the care of a girl	cura puella
17.	return the tablets	tabella reddo
18.	the face of a lover	uultus amans
19.	a blonde girl	flauus puella
20.	things pleasing to a husband	gratus maritus

EXERCISE XX: THE END OF THE LINE II

Translate the following phrases into Latin that will scan as the last two feet of a hexameter line: $- \cup \cup \mid - \overline{\cup}$. Some phrases will scan according to the model of *sidera noctis* ($- \cup \cup \mid - \overline{\cup}$) while others will be like *dona puellae* ($- \cup \mid \cup - \overline{\cup}$). For numbers 16–20, you will have to supply the Latin.

1. horns of the moon   cornu luna
2. temples of the gods   templum deus
3. he wasted years   perdo annus
4. the end of loving   finis amo
5. they tell about battles   proelium narro
6. each one will speak   quisque loquor
7. I will confess the deeds   actum fateor
8. deeds of men   factum vir
9. the letter came   littera venio
10. he admires the arts   suspicio ars
11. weights of iron   pondus ferrum
12. Cupid's mother   mater Amor
13. shadow of a body   corpus umbra
14. divinity of the waters   numen aqua
15. everlasting fame   fama perennis
16. golden-haired Apollo
17. noble river
18. bronze tower
19. sorrowful Achilles
20. grateful Jason

EXERCISE XXI: THE FIRST HEMISTICH

Translate the following phrases into Latin that will scan as the first hemistich (up to the penthemimeral caesura) of a hexameter: $\cup \overline{\cup\cup} \mid - \overline{\cup\cup} \mid -$.

Example: "there was a mudless spring"
fons illimis sum → fons erat illimis ($- \vdots \cup\cup \vdots - - - \parallel$)

1.	he had foretold	uaticinor
2.	Caesar had been seen	uideo Caesar
3.	let him die ungrateful	ingratus occido
4.	I will be carried over long seas	fero per longum fretum
5.	bronze-footed bulls	aeripes taurus
6.	three nights went by	nox tres absum
7.	only the stars are flashing	sidus solum mico
8.	example of crime	exemplum crimen
9.	he wanted to be a god	deus sum uolo
10.	love is a trusting thing	amor res credula sum
11.	there was a royal tower	turris regia sum
12.	night intervened	interuenio nox
13.	the first quiet was at hand	quies prima adsum
14.	sleep holds (their) breasts	somnus pectus habeo
15.	she reaches the king	ad rex peruenio
16.	love induced the crime	amor facinus suadeo
17.	he had been imprisoned by the sea	pelagus claudo
18.	he saw and was dumbfounded	uideo et obstupeo
19.	he believed that they were gods	credo deus sum
20.	"Where are you, Icarus?" he said	Icarus ubi sum dico

EXERCISE XXII: THE SECOND HEMISTICH

Translate the following phrases into Latin that will scan as the second hemistich (after the penthemimeral caesura) of a hexameter: $\overline{\smile\smile} \mid -\overline{\smile\smile} \mid -\smile\smile \mid --$.

Example: "silvery with shining waves"
argenteus unda nitida → nitidis argenteus undis
($\parallel \smile\smile - \mid --\smile\smile \mid --$)

1.	it is the image of royal Jove	imago Iuppiter regalis sum
2.	adorned with small markings	distincta breuis sigillum
3.	more things remain for wretched me	plura misera ego supersum
4.	I also prevail after so many deaths	post tot funus quoque uinco
5.	the goddess addressed her opponents thus	sic dea uetans adfor
6.	I came to the public rites	ad munus publicum uenio
7.	and lifting his hands to the stars	tolloque palma ad sidus
8.	their severed necks are seen	collum interceptum uideo
9.	he sent it into the empty breezes	in aura uacua emitto
10.	and Corinth noble in bronze	et Corinthus nobilis aes
11.	certainly he has moved my heart (pl)	certe moueo pectus meum
12.	and the extinguished flame grew bright again	extinctaque flamma reluceo
13.	he asked with a submissive voice	rogo uox submissa
14.	she speaks with profuse tears	lacrima profusa illa aio
15.	the king himself sat down in the middle	rex ipse medium resedeo
16.	it rises up in a fertile field	in aruum fetum consurgo
17.	they cling with eager embraces	amplexus auidus haereo
18.	and she cooks the black juices	et sucus ater incoquo
19.	why do we sluggish ones now hesitate?	nunc quid iners dubito
20.	thus my fates were leading me	sic fatum meum ego traho

EXERCISE XXIII: ENTIRE HEXAMETERS

The following exercises were written in 1820 by the Rev. Charles Bradley:[48]

The sentences in English are to be translated into Latin verse, by an application of the rules of syntax, as well as of prosody, to the corresponding words in Latin, which follow them: in these exercises a change in the arrangement of the words is not necessary.

1) And now the ambassadors came from the city of Latinus, Crowned with branches of olive, and supplicating favor.

    iamque orator adsum ex urbs Latinus,
    uelatus ramus olea, ueniaque rogans.

2) Scarcely had the next rising day fringed the tops of the mountains with light, When first from the deep ocean the horses of the sun raise themselves, And breathe forth the light of day from their panting nostrils.

    posterus uix summus spargo lumen mons
    ortus dies, cum primum altus sui gurges tollo
    sol equus, luxque elatus naris efflo.

3) Then Mercury took in his hand the wand, by which he had been accustomed to chase away sweet Dreams, and to bring them back again; by which he had been wont to enter the gloomy Regions of the dead, and again to animate the lifeless shades.

    tum dextra uirga insero, qui pello dulcis
    aut suadeo iterum somnus, qui niger subeo
    Tartara, et exsanguis animo assuesco umbra.

---

[48] *Exercises in Latin Prosody and Versification*, 3rd edition (London: A. J. Valpy, 1820). Bradley's directions and English sentences have been reproduced *verbatim*; Latin spellings have been modified to conform with modern practice.

4) The ship, weighted down by the slaughter of the men, and filled with much blood, Receives frequent blows on its curved side: But after it let in the sea at its leaking joints, Filled to its highest parts, is sunk in the waves.

> strages uir* cumulatus ratis, multusque cruor
> plenus, per obliquus creber latus accipio ictus:
> at postquam ruptus pelagus compages haurio,
> ad summus repletus forus, descendo in unda.

> * a syncopated form is required

5) All the grove is shattered; the storms tear off the ancient Branches of the trees; and though for ages penetrated by no Sun, the bowers of shady Lycaeus are laid open.

> omnis nemus frangor; rapio antiqua procella
> bracchia silua; nullusque aspectus per aeuum
> sol, umbrosus pateo aestiua Lycaeus.

EXERCISE XXIV: SENTENCES ACROSS A LINE BREAK

Although the preceding exercises have focused on the composition of various parts of the hexameter line, the line is not the only unit by which words and phrases may be grouped together. Often a phrase will extend from the end of one line to the beginning of the next, not necessarily beginning and ending at caesurae. Translate each of the following phrases so that it will scan across a line break.

Example: "great Atlas is my grandfather"
Atlas maximus auus sum → maximus Atlas / est auus
"maximus Atlas" (– ◡ ◡ ⋮ – –) ends one line, and
"est auus" (– ⋮ ◡ ◡) begins the next

1. she sings a song to help
   carmen auxilio cano
2. and the moist clouds rise
   et nubes umidus surgo
3. he is said to have put down his lyre
   lyra depono fero
4. nor did our love move you
   nec amor noster tu moueo
5. exact the penalties, father Nisus
   poena exigo pater Nisus
6. whom royal Juno turns into a bird
   quae Iuno regia in uolucer uerto
7. and he flies away beating his mangled breast
   lanio pectus plango euolo
8. nevertheless he dies from a small wound
   ille tamen uulnus minimum occido
9. and the wave torn apart by oars resonates
   diuulsaque unda remus sono
10. on the fourth night, the radiant stars flash
    nox quarta sidus radians mico
11. changed into a bird, she is called "Ciris"
    mutata in auis "Ciris" uoco

12. and the plants burn having been touched by the vapors
    tactaque herba uapor ardeo
13. and the rumor of the deed goes through the towns of Phrygia
    Phrygiaque per oppidum eo rumor factum
14. and he bears the weapon (pl.) fixed in the middle of his chest
    mediumque in pectus fixa tela gero
15. and the trembling arrow clung to his upper neck
    summaque ceruix sagitta tremo haereo
16. Phrygian Maeandrus plays in the liquid waves
    Maeandrus Phrygius in unda liquida ludo
17. cruel, he abandoned his companion on that shore
    crudelis comes sua in litus illum destituo
18. she came into Scythia carried through the air on a chariot
    in Scythia subueho per aer currus deuenio
19. and she flies to the threshold of Pelias as a suppliant
    Peliasque ad limen supplex confugio
20. Medea, with her sword drawn, opens up the throat of the old man
    strictus ensis Medea iugulum senis recludo

EXERCISE XXV: SYNONYMS

When composing original poetry, you will often find that a word you would like to use will not scan properly, whether because it is intrinsically unable to fit into a hexameter line (e.g., *ciuitas*, – ∪ –) or because it is metrically incompatible with other words you have written. The ability to come up with appropriate synonyms is thus a crucial skill to develop. Find as many words as you can that are similar in meaning to the thirty English words below. Remember that exact correspondence of meaning is neither required nor possible. For the first example, "large," you might, for instance, consider words meaning "huge," "massive," "great," "big," etc. When you have finished, go back and mark the naturally long and short syllables, and save your work for future reference.

1. large	16. all
2. small	17. pleasant
3. good	18. snake
4. bad	19. bird
5. happy	20. weapon
6. sad	21. defeat
7. go	22. people
8. do	23. friend
9. see	24. god
10. say	25. house
11. give	26. ship
12. take	27. river
13. and	28. sea
14. but	29. water
15. like, as, similar to	30. wind

EXERCISE XXVI: SYNONYMS IN
THE HEXAMETER

The following exercise was devised over 150 years ago by Charles Anthon, and it applies the skill of finding synonyms to specific lines of poetry. In addition it asks you to supply adjectives or "epithets" for certain nouns in order to round out lines that would otherwise be incomplete. Some of the words may also need to be rearranged slightly. Here are Dr. Anthon's exact directions from 1845:

> *In the following Exercises, the Nouns in Italic Characters are to have EPI-THETS adapted to them. The words enclosed within brackets [ ] are to be altered to other SYNONYMOUS terms, the alteration sometimes consisting in a simple change of Number, Case, Mood, or Tense.*[49]

Anthon's own exercises are based on elegiac couplets and will be reserved until a later chapter. The lines below are adapted from Vergil.

Example: [statim] Fama per *urbes* Libyae [incedit]

> *Statim* means "immediately," so *extemplo* and *confestim* would be appropriate synonyms, and they are good transition words that might well start the line. *Libyae* could come next, taking you to the caesura, and *Fama per urbes* looks like a good line ending. *Incedit* has the right number of syllables to fall between *Libyae* and *Fama* but would necessitate a hiatus at the caesura. Furthermore, an adjective for *urbes* is required. *It* is a simple substitute for *incedit*, leaving a spondee for the adjective. There is no need to be exotic; *magnas* or *claras* will suffice, producing the line, *extemplo Libyae magnas it Fama per urbes*. This is exactly what Vergil wrote, but *confestim Libyae claras it Fama per urbes* also scans. Similarly, one could have chosen the nicely vivid verb *ruit*, thereby requiring an adjective beginning with a vowel, perhaps *amplas: extemplo Libyae ruit amplas Fama per urbes*. While it might be profitable to reflect upon the superiority of the Vergilian line, for the purposes of this exercise, anything that scans and makes sense should be considered a "correct" answer.

---

[49] Charles Anthon, *A System of Latin Versification* (New York: Harper & Brothers, 1845) 28.

1. talia [stabat] memorans [et] fixus manebat.
2. Laocoon, [flamen] ductus Neptuno sorte,
   taurum ad sollemnis aras [sacrificabat].
3. ergo iter inceptum [perficiunt] [flumini] que propinquant.
4. rumpe *moras* et arripe *castra*.
5. Turnus at ante uolans [praecessit] *agmen*.
6. *sanguis* in [membra] Arcadibus coit.
7. ergo his dictis [alatum] [Cupidinem] adfatur.
8. [*Saturnia*] urit et sub noctem cura recursat.
9. Turnus [essedo] desiluit, pedes apparat ire
   comminus; utque leo, cum a *specula* [conspexit]
   taurum meditantem in [pugnas] stare procul campis
   [approperat]: haud alia est imago *Turni*.
10. interea Aurora *lucem mortalibus* [induxerat], referens opera [et]
    [luctus]. (2 lines)

SECTION VIII: CIRCUMLOCUTION

Sometimes the use of synonymous words can eliminate metrical difficulties, but other variations will often prove necessary. Indeed, no linguistic skill is more important to the versifier than periphrasis or circumlocution (literally "talking around," i.e. finding a different, and sometimes wordier, way of saying essentially the same thing). The tips below are organized according to the parts of speech, and each point is illustrated by an example and an exercise. [NB: all exercise solutions should be able to stand somewhere in a hexameter line.]

NOUNS AND PRONOUNS

1. Substitute singular for plural and plural for singular, including personal pronouns, e.g., pectus → pectora, os → ora.

    Ex. litus Troiae → _____
         meus Amor → _____

1a. Instead of a simple plural, use collective nouns like *turba, manus, gens*, etc. with the genitive, e.g., uiri → turba uirorum.

    Ex. Rutulians → nation of Rutulians
         Rutuli → _____

2. Use an abstract noun for a concrete noun (and vice versa), e.g., amantes mutabiles sunt → Amor est mutabilis.

    Ex. the brave perish by deceit → bravery (*uirtus*) perishes by deceit
         fortes fraude pereunt → _____

2a. Use an abstract noun for an adjective (and vice versa), e.g., Aeneas furens → furor Aeneae.

    Ex. Turnus superbus → _____

2b. When an abstract noun conveys an action, use a participle, e.g., amissio uirtutis → perdita uirtus.

Ex.   the defeat of the troop → the defeated (*uinco*) troop

     clades cateruae → _____

3. Use a relative clause for a noun, either in the nominative case, e.g., agricola → qui colit agros, or not, e.g., opes Croesi → opes quas Croesus habet.

    Ex.   the failings of my voice → what of my voice was lacking (*desum*)

     defectus uoci →_____

4. Use an infinitive as a noun, e.g., uidere est credere.

    Ex.   to suffer is to learn →_____

5. Use the dative (esp. with *sum*) instead of the genitive or a possessive adjective or the verb *habeo*, e.g., mea nata → nata mihi, domus mea magna est → est mihi magna domus, or vice versa.

    Ex.   amicus Ciceroni→

     mitia poma habemus →

6. Use a vocative instead of the nominative, e.g., Aeolus → Aeole. If the vocative is the same as the nominative (and therefore not a helpful change), add *tu* or an adjective in the vocative, e.g., dea → tu dea, rex magnus → rex magne. Similarly, you may use a verb in the second person instead of the third person: In *Met.* 15, Ovid's Pythagoras asks, "quid meruistis, oves?" (116) because "quid meruere oues?" would not scan as the first hemistich of a hexameter. The vocative may also be used with *tibi* in place of a dative alone, e.g., templum Phoebo sacrauit → templum tibi, Phoebe, sacrauit. Remember that Greek nouns in *-is* have a vocative ending of ï, which can give you a short, open vowel if needed, e.g., "*o crudelis Alexi, nihil mea carmina curas?*"

    Ex.   quidue pater Neptunus parat? →

    _____

    quas poenas mihi Turnus dabit →

    _____

7. Introduce an appositive, e.g., raucae palumbes → raucae, tua cura, palumbes.

    Ex.   grandsons → grandsons, dear offspring (*pignora*)

nepotes → _____

8. Use figures of speech:

   a) synecdoche (the substitution of a part for the whole), especially common with words for "ship," e.g., nauis → carina (keel), prora (prow), puppis (stern).

      Ex. uultus → _____

   b) metonymy (see glossary), e.g., uentus → Boreas, bellum → Mars.

      Ex. frumentum → _____

   c) metaphor (an implied comparison), e.g., consul → gubernator rei publicae

      Ex. Life, to Macbeth, is a "brief candle," a "fitful fever," and a "walking shadow." Translate these examples or devise your own metaphor for life →
      _____

   d) hendiadys (use of two nouns to convey one idea), e.g., hostes insidiosi → hostes insidiaeque

      Ex. pateris aureis libamus → _____

9. Proper names:

   a) Use epithets with the names of gods and heroes, e.g., pius Aeneas, Phoebus Apollo.

      Ex. Jupiter → almighty Jupiter = _____
               Achates → faithful Achates = _____

   b) Use a patronymic (family name, "son/descendant of . . ."), e.g., Achilles → Aeacides (descendant of Aeacus), Juno → Saturnia (daughter of Saturn)

      Ex. Agamemnon (son of Atreus) → _____

   c) Identify a person by some other relationship of blood or friendship, e.g.,

Hercules → Iouis proles, Mercury → Cyllenia proles; Ovid is fond of obscure identifications, e.g., Theseus → Neptunius heros (*Met.* 9.1)

> Ex.   Proserpina → _____
>
> Achaemenides → (companion of unlucky Ulysses)
>
> _____

10. Relative clauses:

   a) The antecedent may be placed within its relative clause, e.g., dona quae pararit → quae dona pararit

   > Ex.   munera quae Dido/fecerat → _____

   b) A relative clause may even precede its antecedent, e.g., et rediit puero, qui fuit ante, color.

   > Ex.   unicus est honor de quo sollicitamur →
   >
   > _____

ADJECTIVES

1. An adjective can sometimes be replaced by a noun in the genitive (see Nouns 2a), e.g., humani preces → preces hominum

   > Ex.   uernaque incertior aura → _____

2. An adjective can be changed into an adverb (and vice versa), e.g., ardens → ardenter.

   > Ex.   suauis → _____
   >
   > aura lenis crepat → _____

3. The superlative or comparative may be used instead of the positive, if sense allows, e.g., fortis heros → fortissimus heros

   > Ex.   cara mater → _____

4. Epithets may be transferred, e.g., change "and the feet of spirited horses" to

"and the spirited feet of horses," quadrupedumque pedes animosorum →
quadrupedumque pedes animosi

> Ex.   the shield of unlucky Euryalus → the unlucky shield of Euryalus
>
> clipeum infelicis Euryali → _____

5. An adjective may be replaced by *non* and an adjective of opposite meaning,
   e.g., paruus → non magnus. *Non* is also effectively used with a negated adjective, e.g., dignus → non indignus. Note, however, that a double negative in
   Latin often suggests an emphatic positive, e.g., non inuitus = "very willing"

> Ex. timidus → _____

5a. *Male* may used in place of *non* or *in-*, e.g., incommodus → male commodus

> Ex.   aeger → _____

5b. *Bene* and *male* may also be used to intensify positive and negative adjectives.

ADVERBS

1. An adverb may be replaced by an adjective modifying the subject (see
   Adjectives 2).

2. Similarly, an adverb may be replaced by an adjective modifying a different
   noun, e.g., magna uoce clamauit

> Ex.   he looked eagerly → he looked with an eager eye
>
> auide spectauit → _____

2a. An ablative absolute may also be used, e.g., sonitu strepitante for "noisily"

> Ex.   rapidly → with quickening step
>
> rapide → _____

3. The ablative of manner may replace an adverb (and vice versa), e.g., cum
   diligentia → diligenter

> Ex.   audis benigne ("with kindness") semper mea uerba, Catulle → _____

VERBS

1. An active verb may be made passive (and vice versa), e.g., hostis mortalis nos
   mortales urget → mortali urgemur ab hoste (*A.* 10.375)

          Ex.   aut hoc lignum Achiuos inclusos occultat →

                 _____

2. A participle may be substituted for a verb, e.g., dona fert → dona ferens

          Ex.   ueniamque rogant → _____

3. A compound verb may be used instead of the simple form (and vice versa), e.g.,
   sequor → persequor

          Ex.   quiesco → _____

   Note that adding a prefix sometimes changes the root verb, e.g., sacro → consecro

          Ex.   iacio → _____

4. If sense allows, the tense of a verb may be changed. Using the historical present
   instead of the perfect is a common substitution, and the imperfect, perfect, and
   pluperfect are sometimes interchanged.

          Ex.   Change the tense of each verb so that it will be able to stand at the
   beginning of a line:
             uenit Aeneas → _____
             cucurrit equus → _____

   A future active participle or future perfect may often be used for a simple future.

          Ex.   Change the verb so the line below will scan:
             progenies caeli magnum ueniet sub axem →

             _____

5. Commands may be expressed in many ways: the imperative mood; the present
   subjunctive; the future; the passive periphrastic; *debet, oportet,* or *necesse est*
   plus the infinitive; and *effice* plus *ut* and the subjunctive.

Ex. Find as many metrically correct solutions as possible for

fac → _____

5a. Negative commands are equally versatile: *ne* plus the subjunctive; *noli* plus the infinitive; *parce, desine, caue, non licet*, etc. plus the infinitive; and *non* and the passive periphrastic.

Ex. Find as many metrically correct solutions as possible for

noli facere → _____

6. The use of a complementary infinitive with verbs like *possum, ualeo*, and *soleo* may be a good way to fill out a line, if sense allows, e.g., sustentat → sustentare ualet

Ex. uincit → _____

PREPOSITIONS

1. Prepositions, despite their name, are often placed after the nouns they govern, e.g., in aduerso pectore → pectore in aduerso

Ex. hoc dicens ferrum sub aduerso pectore condit →

_____

2. The dative of agent may be used instead of *a/ab* plus the ablative (and vice versa), e.g., a te uictus → tibi uictus

Ex. praeteritus a Cerere campus →

_____

3. Note that prepositions are sometimes omitted, even when required in prose.

CONJUNCTIONS

1. *Et* can be omitted (asyndeton).

2. *Et* and *-que* can be postponed, e.g., *mella fluant illi, feret et rubus asper amomum* (*E.* 3.89).

3. In a "both ... and" construction, you may use *et ... et, -que ... -que*, or *-que et*, e.g., fluminaque camposque → fluminaque et campos.

EXTENDED PERIPHRASIS

When writing in the grand style, it is often effective to replace a simple phrase, such as "at dawn" (*prima luce*), with a more elaborate description, e.g., *iam nitidum retegente diem noctisque fugante / tempora Lucifero* (*M.* 8.1–2). Similarly, "the next day" (*proxima die*) can be introduced with the line, *postera depulerat stellas Aurora micantes* (*M.* 7.100), and "on the ninth day" (*nona die*) can become, *nonamque serena / Auroram Phaethonis equi iam luce uehebant* (*A.* 104–5).

Ex.   Create your own periphrasis for a time of day

EXERCISE XXVIIA

Translate the following lines of Pope into Latin hexameters. A paraphrase of the Rev. George Preston's solution is provided.*

> The Fury heard, while on Cocytus' brink
> Her snakes untied sulphureous waters drink;
> But at the summons rolled her eyes around,
> And snatched the startled serpents from the ground,
> Not half so swiftly shoots along the air
> The gliding lightning or descending star;
> Through crowds of airy shades she winged her flight,
> And dark dominions of the silent night:
> Swift as she passed the flitting ghosts withdrew,
> And the pale spectres trembled at her view;
> To the iron gates of Taenarus she flies,
> There spreads her dusky pinions to the skies,
> The day beheld, and sickening at the sight,
> Veiled her fair glories in the shades of night.

> The Fury heard these things while by chance her *disentangled*[1] *snakes*[2]
> Drink *both sulfurs and liquids*[3] on the *bank*[4] of Cocytus:
> *And then,*[5] rolling her eyes around at the warning, the goddess
> Both snatched the *startled*[6] *serpents*[7] *and*[8] lifted them from the ground
> With so swift a *charge*[9] as never across the *air*[10]

---

* Preston's own exercises offer only rather limited assistance, so the passages given here are adapted directly from his *Key to Exercises in Latin Verse*, in this case Part II, Ex. 2.

[1] *explicatus*

[2] *colubra*

[3] *latex* (liquid); use *-que* and *et* for "both . . . and," and note the hendiadys: "sulfurs and liquids" for "sulfurous liquids"

[4] *margin*

[5] *exinde*

[6] *attonitus*

[7] *anguis*

[8] *-que* (postponed)

[9] *impete*

[10] *aethera*

A precipitous force or a path slippery with falling stars drives the *lightning:*[11]
She, amid the spirits, a *crowded throng*[12] without body,
Wanders through the *dismal*[13] night and silent realms.
And no less before her *approach*[14] did the *shades*[15] *give up*[16] their flitting
Columns, and a tremor seizes [their] bloodless limbs at the sight.
From here she *heads for*[17] the Taenarian door posts and *Death's*[18] *iron*[19]
Gates[20] and extends her *dark-blue*[21] wings toward the sun.
The gracious day[22] sees and, bristling at the *sight,*[23] hides [her] honored glory
And is *enveloped*[24] by the *gloomy*[25] shades of night.

[11] place in the previous line
[12] As an appositive, "crowded throng" (*turba crebra*) must agree in case with "spirits."
[13] *intempestus*
[14] *aditus*
[15] *lemures*
[16] *cedo*
[17] *peto*
[18] *Letum*
[19] *ferratum*
[20] *limen*
[21] *liuens*
[22] *dies alma* (place in the next line)
[23] *aspectus*
[24] *inuoluo*
[25] *ater*

EXERCISE XXVIIB

The following exercise was used to determine the University, Exeter, Oriel, Brasenose, and Christ Church Scholarships at Oxford in 1891: Translate the passage below into Latin hexameters. A paraphrase of the Rev. Dr. William Baker's solution is provided although students competing at Oxford over a century ago received no such assistance.

> 'Let him return on board a foreign ship
> And in his house find evil!' Thus he prayed
> With head uplifted and indignant lip;
> And the dark-haired one heeded what he said.
> He there his hand upon a great stone laid,
> Larger by far than that he had hurled before,
> And the huge mass in booming flight obeyed
> The measureless impulse, and right onward bore
> There 'twixt the blue-prowed bark descending and the shore,
> Just short of ruin: and the foaming wave
> Whitened in boiling eddies where it fell,
> And rolling toward the isle our vessel drave,
> Tossed on the waves of that tumultuous swell.
> There found we all our fleet defended well,
> And comrades sorrow-laden on the sand,
> Hoping if yet, past hope, the seas impel
> Their long-lost friends to the forsaken strand.
> Grated our keel ashore: we hurrying leap on land.

"But may he seek again [his] paternal *home*[1] in a *foreign*[2] ship
And may he find *deceit*[3] within the inner *chambers*[4] of [his] house."

---

[1] *sedes* (plural)
[2] *peregrinus*
[3] *fraus*
[4] *penetralia*

Thus he speaks, lifting his indignant face to the stars,
Nor did the father of the *sea*[5] *turn*[6] deaf ears to [his] prayers.
Then *he,*[7] undertaking to surpass prior *blows,*[8]
Lifts up a great rock with great *effort*[9]
And hurls [it]: obeying [his] immense right hand, through the *empty places*[10]
The *mass*[11] flies, and *shrieking,*[12] it seizes a quick course in the *air*[13]
And between the blue-green *ship*[14] and the shore, it *brings on*[15] ruin
With a sound, [and with] a *narrow escape from death.*[16]
But[17] above, the foaming wave *grew white*[18] with swelling
Whirlpools; meanwhile the ship, hurled by a *storm,*[19]
Is carried[20] to the desired *shore*[21] of a *more distant*[22] land.
Here *we*[23] *look over*[24] the ships *made safe*[25] by [our] *defense*[26]
And friends heavy with sadness on a *foreign*[27] *shore,*[28]
Doubtful[29] *amid*[30] *both* hope *and*[31] fear, if by chance

[5] *pelagus*
[6] *applico*
[7] *ille*
[8] *ictus*
[9] *molimen*—note the rhythm of the line
[10] *inania*
[11] *massa*
[12] *strideo*
[13] *aether*
[14] *puppis* (literally the "stern")
[15] *duco* (next line)
[16] *paruum discrimen leti* (idiomatic)
[17] *sed* (postponed)
[18] *incanesco*
[19] *procella*
[20] *fero*
[21] *harena*
[22] *ulterior*
[23] *nos*
[24] *aspicio*
[25] *tutus*
[26] *munimen*
[27] *externus*
[28] *litus*
[29] still agreeing with "friends" above
[30] *inter* (postponed)
[31] *-que . . . -que*

It may be permitted[32] *to behold*[33] [their] *companions,*[34] having been sent away
through the sea[35], *brought back home again.*[36]
The ship *approaches*[37] the shore; the sailors *get hold of*[38] the sand.

<hr/>

[32] *licet* (subj.)
[33] *specto*
[34] *sodalis*
[35] place in previous line
[36] *redux*
[37] *adeo*
[38] *potior* + ablative

EXERCISE XVIIc

The following exercise was used as a scholarship examination at Queen's College, Oxford, in 1889: Translate the passage below into Latin hexameters. A paraphrase is again provided.

> He ended here,
> And to the city full of haughty wrath
> Rushed on, as when yoked to his car a steed,
> For prizes trained, along some level mead
> Pursues with eager stride his easy path;
> So nimbly moved Achilles. As he came,
> Priam's old eyes first saw him from afar
> Across the plain, wide glittering like that star
> In Autumn rising, whose keen rays of flame
> Outshine the crowded orbs, when night is dumb;
> This men the hound of great Orion call,
> An evil sign, though brightest of them all,
> Since great heats with it on frail mortals come.
> Thus as he ran, the brass around his breast
> Flashed fierce and far.

[1]And *having spoken*[2] no more, to the city
He *rushed*,[3] trembling *in his heart*[4] with angry *haughtiness*.[5]
And *just as*,[6] mastered by his chariot, through the grasses of a field
A horse *is carried*,[7] accustomed to run in the grove of Jove,
And, impatient of delay, he seizes an easy course on the *plain*,[8]

---

[1]   begin this line at the penthemimeral caesura
[2]   *effor*
[3]   *irruo*
[4]   *praecordia* (use accusative of respect)
[5]   *fastus*
[6]   *ueluti*
[7]   *fero*
[8]   *aequor*

So *Achilles*[9] moved his steps — [Achilles] whom, *coming*[10]
On the open plain, *old*[11] Priam *first*[12] *recognized*,[13]
Visible[14] *far and wide*,[15] just as when burning Sirius
Rises[16] in Autumn, and with powerful rays
Surpasses all ethereal *orbs*[17] beneath the silent night.
Men *called*[18] this the Dog, a star which *drags*[19] vapors
(*Indeed*[20] [it is] *unlucky*[21] although it shines brightest in the sky)[22]
And immoderate *heat*[23] to wretched mortals;
Just so[24], the youth to be feared in [his] brazen arms
Burned and *blazed*[25] far and wide in [his] *outstanding*[26] splendor.

[9] *Aeacides*, i.e. a "descendant of Aeacus," the grandfather of Achilles
[10] *eo*
[11] *grandaeuus*
[12] place in previous line
[13] *agnosco*
[14] *conspicuus*
[15] *late*
[16] *nascor*
[17] place in previous line
[18] *dico* (use syncopated form)
[19] postpone until line 13
[20] *quidem*
[21] *laeuus*
[22] It is neither unusual nor inelegant for a parenthesis to interrupt a sentence.
[23] *aestus* (plural)
[24] *haud secus*
[25] *reluceo*
[26] *egregius*

EXERCISE XXVIID

Translate the following lines from Milton into Latin hexameters. A paraphrase and notes are provided. Words in brackets are not translated. Remember that the use of "may" plus a verb in English – e.g., "may be able" (3), "may penetrate" (4), "may possess" (8) – requires the subjunctive in Latin.*

>   This having learn'd, thou hast attain'd the sum
>   Of wisdom; hope no higher, though all the stars
>   Thou knew'st by name, and all the ethereal powers,
>   All secrets of the deep, all nature's works,
>   Or works of God in heaven, air, earth, or sea,
>   And all the riches of this world enjoy'dst,
>   And all the rule, one empire; only add
>   Deeds to thy knowledge answerable; add faith,
>   Add virtue, patience, temperance; add love,
>   By name to come call'd Charity, the soul
>   Of all the rest: then wilt thou not be loth
>   To leave this Paradise, but shalt possess
>   A paradise within thee, happier far.

Thus far[1] informed,[2] there is not [any] greater wisdom
Which you *can learn;[3] don't you hope[4]* beyond [it]. All the stars
You may *be able[5]* to *enumerate,[6] as many powers as[7]* rule in the sky;
You may penetrate *also the wonders[8]* of nature, the *mysteries[9]* of the *deep;[10]*

---

   * Adapted from Anthon's *Latin Versification*, Part VI, Ex. 8.
[1] *hactenus*
[2] *edoctus*
[3] *disco* (use subjunctive)
[4] *ne + spero* (subj.)
[5] *queo*
[6] *enarro*
[7] *quot numina*
[8] *miraque*
[9] *arcana*
[10] *profundum*

Whatever[11] God *has created*[12] in the heaven, or in the *firmament*[13] *beneath*[14]
  the heaven,
Through the sea, through the *earth*[15], and in every *world:*[16]
If the sole power of the whole universe *were yours,*[17]
If, *whatever*[18] riches the earth may *possess,*[19] it *bestow*[20] on you alone;
Yet there is a better art and greater *skill;*[21] in [your] deeds
And mind, *equal*[22] [your] fortune. Let Patience *gather strength,*[23]
Let [your] faith *shine forth*[24] *more firm*[25] and [your] virtue more increased;
Apply[26] a *curb*[27] to depraved desires and senses.
Nor let *that*[28] love be wanting unto you, which [is] dear *to all,*[29]
Which believes that nothing human *does not belong*[30] to itself.
Hence you will *depart*[31] *from*[32] Elysium not unwilling,
For you will have Elysium, *how much*[33] *more happy,*[34] within.

[11] *quid*
[12] *creo* (perf. subj.), use in next line
[13] *aethra*
[14] *subter*
[15] *terra*, use poetic plural
[16] *orbis*
[17] *tua* + pres. subj. of *sum*
[18] *quot*
[19] *habeo*
[20] *defero* (subj.)
[21] *peritia*
[22] use subjunctive, i.e. "you should equal . . ."
[23] *cresco*
[24] *nitesco*
[25] *firma magis* (not necessarily next to each other)
[26] *addo* (use subjunctive, "you should add . . .")
[27] *frenum* (use plural)
[28] *iste*
[29] *in omnes*
[30] *non interfore*
[31] *abeo*
[32] *ex*
[33] *quantus*
[34] *felicius*

EXERCISE XXVIIE

The translation of religious literature into Latin is a significant part of the tradition of Latin verse composition. Translate the 98th Psalm into hexameters. A paraphrase is provided.*

> O sing to the Lord a new song, for he has done marvelous things.
>> His right hand and his holy arm have gotten him victory.
> The Lord has made known his victory;
>> he has revealed his vindication in the sight of the nations.
> He has remembered his steadfast love and faithfulness to the house of Israel.
>> All the ends of the earth have seen the victory of God.
> Make a joyful noise to the Lord, all the earth;
>> break forth into joyous song and sing praises.
> Sing praises to the Lord with the lyre,
>> with the lyre and the sound of melody.
> With trumpets and the sound of the horn
>> make a joyful noise before the King, the Lord.
> Let the sea roar, and all that fills it;
>> the world and those who live in it.
> Let the floods clap their hands;
>> let the hills sing together for joy
> At the presence of the Lord, for he is coming to judge the earth.
>> He will judge the world with righteousness, and the peoples with equity.†

> Let Jehovah be celebrated with praise *unheard before;*[1]
> Let the grateful earth sing of [its] creator: all *wonders*[2]
> *He*[3] *does,*[4] *his own strength,*[5] and [his] right hand the triumph

---

* Adapted from Charles Anthon's *Latin Versification*, Part VI, Ex. 12.
† The English translation of the psalm is taken from the New Revised Standard Version of the Bible.
[1] *non prius audita*
[2] *mira*
[3] *ille*
[4] *facio*
[5] *propriae uires*

has gained.[6] Lo, he has *shown forth*[7] [his] *salvation*[8] in the whole
world;[9]

He has *shown*[10] himself holy to the *unbelievers*,[11] himself just to the
unrighteous.[12]

His own *people*[13] now *know*[14] that ever of *truth*[15] and *equity*[16]

And [his] promise, God is *mindful*[17]; and in all *lands*[18]

The *alien people*[19] see how great salvation, if *he himself wills it*,[20]

He can effect, [and] what great *strength*[21] he can give to [his] *beloved
nation.*[22]

Therefore, let the sound of *gladness*[23] *arise*[24] *over*[25] all

Lands; let them testify their love to God with a grateful voice:

And let the harps resound, let the hymn respond to the harps:

Let the horns *mingled*[26] with the *trumpet*[27] celebrate the *everlasting*[28]
king.

Let the *sea*,[29] and whatever *tribe*[30] *floats upon*[31] the water *of the sea,*[32]

[6] *refero*
[7] *monstro*
[8] *salus*
[9] *orbis*
[10] *ostendo*
[11] *infidus*
[12] *iniquus*
[13] *gens sua*
[14] *noui*
[15] *uerum*
[16] *aequum*
[17] *memor*
[18] *ora*
[19] *gens aliena*
[20] *ipse uolo* (subj.)
[21] *robor*
[22] *populus amatus*
[23] *laetitia*
[24] *exorior*
[25] *in*
[26] *mixtus*
[27] *tuba*
[28] *aeternus*
[29] *aequor*
[30] *genus*
[31] *innato* + ablative
[32] *aequoreus*

Let the *world*[33], and *wherever*[34] in the *extended*[35] world *men dwell,*[36]
Shout loudly,[37] and let the waves *roar,*[38] and the hills *re-echo;*[39]
For[40] the Lord is coming *to judge*[41] all lands;
God himself *is coming*[42] *to*[43] *give*[44] *mild*[45] *laws*[46] to the various nations,
And *restrain*[47] the *people*[48] under [his] equal *rule.*[49]

[33] *orbis*
[34] *quacumque*
[35] *extentus*
[36] *habitatur* (impersonal)
[37] *affremo*
[38] *reboo*
[39] *resulto*
[40] *quippe*
[41] *ut + iudico* (subj.)
[42] *aduenio*
[43] *ut* + subjunctive
[44] place in the next line
[45] *almus*
[46] place in the next line
[47] *coerceo*
[48] use plural
[49] *lex*

EXERCISE XXVIIF

The following passage was used for a scholarship examination at Queen's College, Oxford, in 1891. Try to translate these lines into hexameters without the aid of a paraphrase.

> What though for him no Hybla sweets distil,
> Nor bloomy vines wave purple on the hill;
> Tell that when silent years have passed away,
> That when his eyes grow dim, his tresses grey,
> These busy hands a lovelier cot shall build,
> And deck with fairer flowers his little field,
> And call from heaven propitious dews to breathe
> Arcadian beauty on the barren heath:
> Tell that while love's spontaneous smile endears
> The days of peace, the sabbath of his years,
> Health shall prolong to many a festive hour
> The sacred pleasures of his humble bower.

EXERCISE XXVIII — LATIN
TRANSLATIONS OF ENGLISH POEMS

Before composing completely original poetry, it is beneficial first to rendering some English poetry into Latin hexameters. This exercise eliminates the need to decide *what to say* and focuses instead on determining *how to say it*. All the principles of versification – from elementary scansion to rhythms and verbal effects to finding synonyms, epithets and other means of circumlocution – must now be brought into play. While your hexameter translation should strive to capture the meaning, style, and tone of the English poem as accurately as possible, remember that your first and most important goal is to produce sensible, metrically correct Latin verses.

Several suggested poems are printed below, but any other poems you like, including the lyrics to popular songs, can serve the purpose of this assignment equally well. More advanced students may even wish to translate a Greek poem into Latin, an exercise as old as the Roman poets themselves.

1. Pope, from *An Essay on Criticism*

    Learning and Rome alike in empire grew;
    And arts still followed where her eagles flew;
    From the same foes, at last, both felt their doom,
    And the same age saw learning fall, and Rome.

2. Blake, "The Lilly"

    The modest Rose puts forth a thorn,
    The humble Sheep a threat'ning horn;
    While the Lilly white shall in Love delight,
    Nor a thorn, nor a threat, stain her beauty bright.

3. Tennyson, "The Eagle"

    He clasps the crag with crooked hands;
    Close to the sun in lonely lands,
    Ringed with the azure world he stands.

The wrinkled sea beneath him crawls;
He watches from his mountain walls,
And like a thunderbolt he falls.

4. Dryden, "Epigram on Milton"[1]

Three *Poets* in three distant *Ages* born,
Greece, Italy and *England* did adorn.
The *First* in loftiness of thought Surpass'd;
The *Next* in Majesty; in both the *Last*.
The force of *Nature* cou'd no farther goe:
To make a *Third* she joynd the former two.

5. Dryden, from "Alexander's Feast"

"Revenge, revenge!" Timotheus cries,
"See the Furies arise!
See the snakes that they rear,
How they hiss in their hair,
And the sparkles that flash from their eyes!"

6. Donne, "Hero and Leander"

Both robbed of air, we both lie in one ground,
Both whom one fire had burnt, one water drowned.

7. Donne, "Pyramus and Thisbe"

Two, by themselves, each other, love and fear
Slain, cruel friends, by parting have joined here.

8. Donne, "Niobe"

By children's births, and death, I am become
So dry, that I am now mine own sad tomb.

[1] The poet Hopkins once translated this epigram into Latin hexameters.

9. Shelley, "Love's Philosophy"

> The fountains mingle with the river,
> And the rivers with the ocean,
> The winds of heaven mix for ever
> With a sweet emotion.
> Nothing in the world is single,
> All things by a law divine
> In one another's being mingle,
> Why not I with thine?
>
> See the mountains kiss high heaven
> And the waves clasp one another;
> No sister flower would be forgiven
> If it disdained its brother:
> And the sunlight clasps the earth,
> And the moonbeams kiss the sea;
> What are all these kissings worth
> If thou kiss not me?

10. Yeats, "Leda and the Swan"

> A sudden blow: the great wings beating still
> Above the staggering girl, her thighs caressed
> By the dark webs, her nape caught in his bill,
> He holds her helpless breast upon his breast.
>
> How can those terrified vague fingers push
> The feathered glory from her loosening thighs?
> And how can body, laid in that white rush,
> But feel the strange heart beating where it lies?
>
> A shudder in the loins engenders there
> The broken wall, the burning roof and tower
> And Agamemnon dead.
> Being so caught up,
> So mastered by the brute blood of the air,
> Did she put on his knowledge with his power
> Before the indifferent beak could let her drop?

11. Milton, "Methought I saw . . ."

> Methought I saw my late espoused Saint
> Brought to me like *Alcestis* from the grave,
> Whom *Jove's* great son to her glad Husband gave,
> Rescu'd from death by force though pale and faint.
> Mine as whom washt from spot of child-bed taint,
> Purification in the old Law did save,
> And such, as yet once more I trust to have
> Full sight of her in Heaven without restraint,
> Came vested all in white, pure as her mind:
> Her face was vail'd, yet to my fancied sight,
> Love, sweetness, goodness, in her person shin'd
> So clear, as in no face with more delight.
> But O as to embrace me she enclin'd
> I wak'd, she fled, and day brought back my night.

12. Shakespeare, Sonnet 73

> That time of year thou mayst in me behold
> When yellow leaves, or none, or few, do hang
> Upon those boughs which shake against the cold,
> Bare ruin'd choirs where late the sweet birds sang.
> In me thou see'st the twilight of such day
> As after sunset fadeth in the west,
> Which by and by black night doth take away,
> Death's second self, that seals up all in rest.
> In me thou see'st the glowing of such fire,
> That on the ashes of his youth doth lie,
> As the death-bed whereon it must expire,
> Consum'd with that which it was nourish'd by.
> This thou perceiv'st, which makes thy love more strong,
> To love that well which thou must leave ere long.

13. Spenser, Sonnet 75 from *Amoretti*

> One day I wrote her name upon the strand;
> But came the waves and washed it away:
> Again, I wrote it with a second hand;
> But came the tide, and made my pains his prey.

Vain man, said she, that dost in vain assay
A mortal thing so to immortalize;
For I myself shall like to this decay,
And eke my name be wiped out likewise.
Not so, quoth I; let baser things devise
To die in dust, but you shall live by fame:
My verse your virtues rare shall eternize,
And in the heavens write your glorious name.
Where, whenas death shall all the world subdue,
Our love shall live, and later life renew.

14. Try some light verse: Burgess, "The Purple Cow"

I never saw a Purple Cow,
I never hope to see one;
But I can tell you, anyhow,
I'd rather see than be one.
Ah, yes! I wrote the "Purple Cow" –
I'm sorry, now, I wrote it!
But I can tell you, anyhow,
I'll kill you if you quote it!

15. Can you make poetry out of this?[2]

Persons advertising in the *Standard* can now have the answers
addressed free of charge at our offices, 23 St. Bride's Street, E.C. If
the answers are to be forwarded, stamps sufficient to cover the post-
age must be sent with the advertisement.

---

[2] From George Preston's *Exercises in Latin Verse* (1889).

SECTION IX: THE ELEGIAC METER

Once the hexameter has been mastered, it is relatively easy to acquire facility in other meters, and the elegiac distich or "couplet" is a logical next step, for it consists of a dactylic hexameter and a pentameter, a line of five (πέντε) dactylic feet, or, more precisely, two units of 2½ feet each. Since the rules of prosody do not change from meter to meter, learning to write elegiacs is simply a matter of becoming familiar with the rules and pecularities of a new metrical pattern and then trying to achieve the maximum rhythmic variety within the constraints of the meter. All of the other, finer points about writing Latin poetry will continue to serve you as you learn this and other new meters.

The elegiac meter putatively takes its name from the Greek words ἒ ἒ λέγειν (to say 'alas, alas') and is therefore often associated with sad subjects. Ovid, for instance, used the meter both for his love elegies (poems about the sufferings of a lover) and for his sorrowful exile poetry. But not all poetry written in elegiac couplets has a sad theme, and amatory or erotic overtones often predominate, especially in the hands of Ovid, who used elegiacs for his mock-didactic *Art of Love* and for the *Fasti*, a poem ostensibly about the Roman calendar but not without its share of love stories. Furthermore, the Romans also composed epigrams and other occasional pieces in the elegiac meter, which was considered less grand and dignified than the stately hexameter. Modern practice continues to reflect this ancient diversity.

The hexameter of the elegiac couplet is formed in exactly the manner you have already learned, while the pentameter has the following shape:

$$- \overline{\smile\smile} \mid - \overline{\smile\smile} \mid - \| - \smile\smile \mid - \smile\smile \mid \overset{\smile}{\smile}.$$

Notice that spondees may be substituted for the two dactyls of the first hemistich, but no such substitutions are allowed in the second half. Conversely, while the line may end with either a short or a long syllable (the long being the more common), the final syllable of the first hemistich *must* be long. The strong caesura after 2½ feet is also mandatory and inflexible. Several other guidelines should be observed as well:

1) The pentameter almost always ends with a word of two syllables, sometimes combined with the prodelision of *est* (e.g., *sua est*). While exceptions to this rule are more frequent in Latin elegy than most verse guides would have us suppose, the disyllabic ending is by far the most common, especially if we follow the model of Ovid's pre-exile poetry.

Because of their relative rarity, polysyllabic endings can add variety, elegance, and grandeur to a line. Such is the case in Cat. 68.112, *audit falsiparens Amphitryoniades*, where a seven-syllable patronymic for Hercules makes this impressive three-word pentameter "one of the most Greek sounding lines in Latin" (Fordyce 356). A monosyllable and a six-syllable word in combination can achieve a similar effect, as in Ovid's *Ibis: sis Berecynthiades* (508). Quadri- and quinquesyllablic endings, although still fairly rare, are a bit more common and therefore do not always carry any special meaning, e.g., *Pars ego sum uestrae proxima militiae* (*Prop.* 1.21.4). Sometimes, however, they are used to good literary effect. In *Heroides* 19, Hero concludes her account of a dream with a line that ends in a four-syllable word: *unda simul miserum uitaque deseruit* (202). Here, "the metrical anomaly is no casual aberration: it underlines the message of the word itself, the tragic isolation of this doomed heroine". Similarly, the unusual rhythm of *Fast.* 6.660, *Cantabat maestis tibia funeribus*, may reflect the mournful sounds of the flute.[1] There are also cases like *Fasti* 5.582: *et circumfusis inuia fluminibus*. Although the quadrisyllabic ending may have no particular point in and of itself, the placement of *fluminibus* at the end of the line allows the Parthian nation to be made graphically "inaccessable" (*inuia*) since it is enveloped by "surrounding rivers" (*circumfusis . . . fluminibus*). The trisyllabic ending is quite rare, especially if we follow Platnauer's analysis and regard phrases like *in foliis* (Prop. 2.20.6) and *et Calais* (1.20.26) as essentially quadrisyllabic: there are twenty in Tibullus, thirty in Propertius, and only three in Ovid.[2] In light of these examples, the modern composer needs to make a conscious stylistic choice. If an Ovidian style is your goal, avoid trisyllabic pentameter endings entirely[3] and restrict four- and five-syllable endings to passages in which they may bear some special effect or emphasis. If, on the other hand, the neoteric verse technique of Catullus is to be your stylistic model, a freer inclusion of a variety of polysyllabic endings is warranted. And if you prefer Tibullus or the early works of Propertius, make the disyllable your norm but don't shy away from the occasional polysyllabic ending, especially the quadrisyllable.[4]

---

[1] Kenney (1996) 22.

[2] Platnauer 15–16.

[3] Ovid's three examples are spread out over more than 10,000 pentameters. Unless you are planning to write a few thousand elegiac couplets, avoid the trisyllabic pentameter ending if writing in Ovid's style.

[4] Postgate 85 observes that "the proportion of Disyllabic endings to the rest rises

1a) Monosyllables may end the line only when they cause an elision (e.g., *mea est*), and exceptions are quite rare. When they do occur, the final two words of the line are almost always closely linked, e.g., *sat est* (*Trist.* 5.7.68), *factaque sunt* (Cat. 76.8), and *et hoc* (Martial 7.10.12).[5] Similarly, monosyllables typically end the first hemistich of the pentameter only when involved in an elision (*non haec ut fama est, A.A.* 1.258), but they may also be acceptable here if preceded by another monosyllable (e.g., *ante frequens quo sit, A.A* 1.150) or a disyllable (*cumque pater tibi sit, A.A.* 1.196).

2) Although the final disyllable of the pentameter may potentially be preceded by almost any combination of words from *excutiatque faces* (– ∪ ∪ – ∪ ⋮ ∪ –) to *tu mihi sola places* (– ⋮ ∪ ∪ ⋮ – ∪ ⋮ ∪ –), the most common pentameter endings follow the models of *carmine doctus amet* (– ∪∪ ⋮ – ∪ ⋮ ∪ ∪) and *arte regendus Amor* (– ∪ ⋮ ∪ – ∪ ⋮ ∪ ∪). Accordingly, these patterns are generally avoided in the first hemistich of either the pentameter or the hexameter, both to achieve the greatest variety possible within a fairly rigid form and to preserve a regular close for the couplet (and notice how the coincidence of accent and vowel quantity in the first two words contributes to the sense of closure). When the principle is violated, it is often to achieve some special effect, e.g., the notorious *semibouemque uirum semiuirumque bouem* (*A.A.* 2.24) in which the double transposition of *bouem* and *uirum* describes the Minotaur with a witty play on words.[6] Similarly, in the refrain of *Amores* 1.6, *tempora noctis eunt; excute poste seram*, the metrical pattern – ∪∪ ⋮ – ∪ ⋮ ∪ ∪ is repeated in both halves of the pentameter to create the sound of a jingle or magic charm to persuade the doorkeeper to admit the frustrated lover.[7] Where no

steadily from Catullus to Ovid," and Platnauer 17 finds a substantial 166 quadrisyllabic endings in Propertius.

[5] Additional examples include Ovid, *P.* 6.26; Martial 1.32.2, 7.10.14, 7.75.2, 10.16.8, 12.47.2, and 12.68.6. See Platnauer 24 and Postgate 86.

[6] Such verbal repetition is characteristic of the Ovidian style, and to my ear it has a certain charm. Who but Ovid would dare to write *tergeminumque uirum tergeminumque canem ... centimanumque Gygen semibovemque uirum* (*T.* 4.7.16, 18), *cedere iussit aquam: iussa recessit aqua* (*Am.* 3.6.44), or *et gelidum Borean egelidumque Notum* (2.11.10)? [Seneca has a famous and funny story about these lines at *Contr.* 2.2.12.] And who but Ovid would repeat *militat omnis amans* in both the first hemistich of the hexameter and the second hemistich of the pentameter in the same couplet? [For more examples and an analysis of the poetic effects of such παρομοίωσις in context, see McKeown on *Amores* 1.9.1–2, 2.11.10, and (soon, one hopes) 3.6.44).]

[7] See McKeown *ad loc.*, who notes that "only fifteen pentameters in the *Amores* (i.e.

particular effect is intended, it is generally better for the first hemistich of the pentameter to be entirely unable to stand in the second half, either because it contains one or more spondees, e.g., *alter et hic mensis, ⁞ sic liber alter eat* (*Fast.* 2.2), or because it ends with a word of three or more syllables, e.g., *exiguum, memini, ⁞ nuper eratis opus* (4).

3) The final word of the pentameter is usually either a noun or a verb,[8] although a pronoun is not uncommon.[9] Adverbs, conjunctions, numerals, and adjectives are comparatively rare.[10]

4) Although the last syllable of the pentameter may be long or short, a short open vowel is rarely allowed to stand at the end of the line, and ĕ is more common than ă.[11]

5) While elision at the caesura of the hexameter is not uncommon, it is extremely rare at the pentameter caesura and should be avoided. The only examples I can find are Catullus 75.4, *nec desistere amare omnia si facias*, Prop. 1.5.32, *quaerere non impune illa rogata uenit*, and 3.22.10, *Herculis Antaeique Hesperidumque choros*. Ovid, however, seems to have disliked the effect, for he changed the line to *Herculis ante oculos uirgineumque chorum* at *A.A.* 3.168.

6) Vowel lengthening at the caesura is no less common in the hexameter of an elegiac couplet than it is in the dactylic hexameter alone, and the principles described in section V, 5 above are equally relevant to elegiacs. Somewhat less common is vowel lengthening at the pentameter caesura. Propertius writes *uinceris aut uincis haec in amore rota est* (2.8.8), and *aut pudor ingenuus, aut reticendus amor* (2.24.4), but textual questions have been raised about both of these lines. There are eight instances in Ovid, all of which involve the lengthening of *i* in the third person singular perfect indicative to reflect an older quantity, e.g., *hac Helle periit, hac ego laedor aqua* (*Her.* 19.128).[12]

7) The couplet: In the elegiac meter, the couplet is the basic unit of composition. Often the hexameter and pentameter combine to form a single thought, e.g.,

barely more than 1%) contain words of a matching numerical sequence of syllables in both hemistichs."

[8] Platnauer 40 calcluates the frequency of such endings to be approximately 80%.
[9] Platnauer's statistic is 17%.
[10] See Platnauer 41–48 for an analysis.
[11] Lupton, *Elegiac Verse* 38.
[12] See Platnauer 60 for the complete list.

> Sic ubi fata uocant, udis abiectus in herbis
> ad uada Maeandri concinit albus olor (*Her.* 7.1–2).

Alternatively, each line may be a single sentence unto itself, e.g.,

> Aestus erat mediamque dies exegerat horam;
> apposui medio membra leuanda toro (*Am.* 1.5.1–2),

or the couplet could consist of two or more sentences with sense breaks falling at any position in either line, e.g.,

> arguet: arguito; quicquid probat illa, probato;
> quod dicet, dicas; quod negat illa, neges (*A.A.* 2.199–200).

When the hexameter is not a complete sentence or clause, the most frequent type of enjambment involves a single dactylic word, e.g., *lite uacent aures, insanaque protinus absint / iurgia* (*Fast.* 1.73–4). As in the dactylic hexameter, an enjambed dactyl in the pentameter can convey the sense of sudden force or motion, e.g., *nam siue aetherias uicino sole per auras / ibimus* (*AA* 2.59–60). Other rhythmic patterns can be equally effective, and a pause after the spondaic first foot of a pentameter can provide a sense of grandeur or gravity, e.g., *nulla Mycenaeum sociasse cubilia mecum / iuro* (*Her.* 3.109–110). Indeed, since Ovid much prefers to begin his pentameters with a dactyl, any spondaic opening can convey a certain *gravitas*, as in the stately, epic apostrophe of *et uos, Nisaei, naufraga monstra, canes* (*Fast.* 4.500). Very rarely does the sense of one couplet extend into the next, and if the couplet does not end at a full stop, it will at least mark the end of a major clause or other logical unit of sense. Even in these instances, however, the spill-over from couplet to couplet will often bear special emphasis, e.g.,*Am.* 1.8.109ff. in which a four-line sentence "expresses Ovid's difficulty in restraining himself from attacking Dipsas."[13] True enjambment from pentameter to hexameter would break the concept of the couplet as the basic sense-unit and should therefore be carefully avoided unless some special effect is intended; even then great restraint is called for. Propertius 4.8.68–69 is a rare and very effective example in which Lygdamus is suddenly discovered hiding behind a couch: *Lygdamus ad plutei fulcra sinistra latens / eruitur.*

---

[13] McKeown (1987) 111.

EXERCISE XXIX: ELEGIAC SCANSION

Scan the following Ovidian elegy (*Ex Ponto* 2.6), marking caesurae and noting elisions when they occur. Other subtleties of versification such as rhythmic variation, word order, and the position of sense breaks within and between couplets should also be observed.

Carmine Graecinum, qui praesens uoce solebat,
    tristis ab Euxinis Naso salutat aquis.
exulis haec uox est: praebet mihi littera linguam
    et, si non liceat scribere, mutus ero.
corripis, ut debes, stulti peccata sodalis
    et mala me meritis ferre minora doces.
uera facis, sed sera meae conuicia culpae:
    aspera confesso uerba remitte reo.
cum poteram recto transire Ceraunia uelo,
    ut fera uitarem saxa monendus eram.
nunc mihi naufragio quid prodest discere facto
    qua mea debuerit currere cumba uia?
bracchia da lasso potius prendenda natanti
    nec pigeat mento subposuisse manum.
idque facis faciasque precor: sic mater et uxor,
    sic tibi sint fratres totaque salua domus,
quodque soles animo semper, quod uoce precari,
    omnia Caesaribus sic tua facta probes.
turpe erit in miseris ueteri tibi rebus amico
    auxilium nulla parte tulisse tuum,
turpe referre pedem nec passu stare tenaci,
    turpe laborantem deseruisse ratem,
turpe sequi casum et Fortunae accedere amicum
    et, nisi sit felix, esse negare suum.
non ita uixerunt Strophio atque Agamemnone nati,
    non haec Aegidae Pirithoique fides.
quos prior est mirata, sequens mirabitur aetas,
    in quorum plausus tota theatra sonant.
tu quoque per durum seruato tempus amico

dignus es in tantis nomen habere uiris,
dignus es, et, quoniam laudem pietate mereris,
    non erit officii gratia surda tui.
crede mihi, nostrum si non mortale futurum est
    carmen, in ore frequens posteritatis eris.
fac modo permaneas lasso, Graecine, fidelis
    duret et in longas impetus iste moras.
quae tu cum praestes, remo tamen utor in aura,
    nec nocet admisso subdere calcar equo.

EXERCISE XXX: JUMBLED PENTAMETERS

Rearrange the following sentences to form proper pentameter lines. There are no elisions. In some cases, more than one solution is possible.

1. ferae auidae uiscera nostra diripiunt
2. illa ruina prima meae mentis fuit
3. amor legitimus pectora casta momordit
4. ab urbe sua cessit coniunx ipsa Iouis
5. hoc pia lingua hoc libertas mihi dedit
6. Cytherea te thalamo meo pollicita est
7. una flamma rogi meas flammas finiet
8. mandantis uiri simplicitate utere
9. meo iudicio ipse uir ueniam dabit
10. sit nulla gratia debita facto meo
11. causa est non satis liquido cognita mihi
12. priore mense tuas partes distuleram
13. fessa labore ad fores nostras restitit
14. ait, "nymphe, posse nescio quid uideris"
15. Alcides Haemoniusque puer adgemit
16. regia Iouis Stygii saepe tibi uisa est
17. umbra lubrica manus prensantes effugit
18. aequoreus deus prima pocula accipit
19. Mars uenit et signa bellica ueniens dedit
20. uouerat et redit laetus ab hoste fuso
21. gentes deuictae nil ualent in amore
22. tamen illa ferrea numquam "amo" dixit
23. femina hoc unum opus semper discit
24. nouit uerus amor nullum modum habere
25. nemo non nocuisse absenti uelit

99

EXERCISE XXXI: JUMBLED COUPLETS

Rearrange the following sentences to form complete elegiac couplets. In some cases more than one solution is possible. Notice that in this exercise the enclitic *-que* appears by itself, indicating that it should not necessarily be attached to the word that immediately precedes it but rather to whatever word is placed first in its clause when the couplet is correctly rearranged. Thus, in couplet 1, the *-que* could be attached to *Melanthius, actor, pecoris*, or *edendi*. This additional challenge may prove difficult, but it is a necessary step along the path to original verse composition.

1. Irus egens Melanthius -que actor pecoris edendi in tua damna accendunt ultimus pudor

2. gloria non est operosa credentem puellam fallere; fuit digna fauore simplicitas

3. herba saepe sustinuit Venerem creatum -que Cinyra sub ilicibus quaelibet positos duos

4. uenefica barbara narratur uenisse tecum recepta in parte tori promissi mihi

5. illa meis pignoribus parceret quae corpora fratris lacerata per agros spargere potuit

6. iamque longum hydram nigris unguibus satur refert redit -que ad dominum refert -que ficta uerba

7. est lacus, sacer antiqua religione, praecinctus opaca silua uallis Aricinae

8. fieri iubet Veneri templa, quibus factis ordine inde tenet Venus nomina corde uerso

9. sanguis Lernaeae echidnae mixtus sanguine Centauri dabat nulla tempora ad auxilium

10. coniugio peracto mercede sceleris Tullia uirum exstimulare his dictis solita est

EXERCISE XXXII: THE END OF THE PENTAMETER

While the composition of the hexameter and the first hemistich of the pentameter will be familiar to you from previous exercises, it is worth practicing the end of the pentameter before attempting the entire couplet. The following models will apply:

1–10	$-\cup\cup \mid -\cup \mid \cup \bar{\cup}$	carmine doctus amet
11–20	$-\cup \mid \cup -\cup \mid \cup \bar{\cup}$	arte regendus Amor

1.	(it is) shameful to win, men	turpe uinco uir
2.	from that place nothing is lost	inde nihil depereo
3.	a gentle breeze leads (us) on	aura leuis proueho
4.	she was the wife of a soldier	uxor miles sum
5.	suited to my habits	apta mos meus
6.	each ensuing day	quaeque dies proxima
7.	the wind stirs up the waves	auster aqua concito
8.	and sluggish winter fled	pigraque hiems fugio
9.	the wool was dirty	lana sordida sum
10.	my heart (pl.) lies open	pectus nostrum pateo
11.	of your death, Dido	mors tua Elissa
12.	the hour is able to return	hora possum redeo
13.	the field grows old from the harvest	ager messis senesco
14.	(her) hands both give and deny	manus do nego
15.	a beauty-patch veils her cheeks	aluta gena uelo
16.	(my) writings will be given to the waves	scriptum aqua do
17.	let down (sing.) your hair often	saepe coma resoluo
18.	love is often prepared	saepe amor paro
19.	the horse (was) compelled to go	equus eo coago
20.	no trust was left	fides nulla relinquo

EXERCISE XXXIII: THE FULL COUPLET

Using the vocabulary provided, translate the following sentences into elegiac couplets. The line breaks have been identified for you in examples 1–5 but not in 6–10. Some rearrangement of the words is required in all exercises.

1. There is nothing but sea and air wherever I look –
   the one swollen with waves, the other threatening with clouds.

   nihil sum nisi pontus et aer quocumque aspicio,
       hic tumidus fluctus, ille minax nubes

2. But poor Elpenor, having fallen from a high roof,
   ran into his king as a crippled shade.

   at Elpenor miser delapsus a(b) tectum altum
       occurro rex suus umbra debilis

3. Add the fact that my talent, weakened by extensive rustiness,
   is sluggish, and it is much less than what it was before.

   addo quod ingenium laesum longa rubigo
       torpeo et sum multo minus quam ante sum

4. Leisure (pl.) nourishes the body; the mind is also fed by it.
   Excessive labor, on the other hand, plucks away at both.

   alo otia corpus, quoque animus illa pascor;
       contra immodicus labor utrumque carpo

5. Whenever Jupiter delights the fields with useful showers,
   the tough burr is accustomed to grow mixed in with the crops.

   quotiens Iuppiter agri imbres utiles iuuo,
       tenax lappa mixta seges cresco soleo.

102

6. And nevertheless my Muse, a friend amid such misfortunes, is strong to return to her rhythms and sacred rites.

   et tamen Musa, hospita in tanta mala, sustineo reuertor ad numeri antiqua -que sacra

7. Even that abandoned Achilles allowed his arms to be idle among the Trojans when his spouse was taken away.

   etiam ille desertus Achilles perfero arma sua in Teucri cesso coniunx abrepta

8. They say that Orpheus soothed wild beasts and restrained agitated rivers with his Thracian lyre.

   dico Orpheus (acc. = Orphea) delenio ferae et flumina concita Threicia lyra sustineo

9. Timid, I have become accustomed to endure all commands of an overbearing woman and not to complain about her deeds in piercing grief.

   consuesco timidus perfero iussa omnia superba neque queror facta argutus dolor

10. I have not fallen more lightly than he whom Jupiter drove back from Thebes with his fire for saying boastful things (*magna*).

    nec ille leuius cado, qui magna locutus Iuppiter a Thebae ignis suus repello

EXERCISE XXXIVA

Translate the following lines by George Lamb into elegiac couplets. A paraphrase and notes based on the Rev. George Preston's solution are provided.*

> Rest, weary stranger, in this shady cave,
> And taste, if languid, of the mineral wave,
> There's virtue in the draught, for health, that flies
> From crowded cities and their smoky skies,
> Here lends her power to every grove and hill,
> Strength to the breeze, and medicine to the rill.

Halt[1] [your] steps under the cover of a cave, tired traveler,
For[2] here you may drink from the *healing*[3] stream [if] languid;
It will have been profitable to have *tasted.*[4] *Health*[5] *which flees*[6]
A sky black with soot[7] and [flees] the *crowded*[8] paths of the city,
Here *freely*[9] *accommodates*[10] herself to every mountain and forest;
From here[11] there is vigor for the winds, here medicine[12] for the water.

---

* Adapted from *Exercises in Latin Verse*, p. 1.
[1] *sisto*
[2] *licet*
[3] *medicus*
[4] *gusto* (use the syncopated form of the perfect infinitive)
[5] *Hygia*
[6] place "health which flees" in the next line
[7] place in the previous line; "soot" is *"fuligo"*
[8] *densus*
[9] *libens*
[10] *commodo*
[11] *hinc*
[12] *medicamen*

EXERCISE XXXIVB

Translate the following lines by Samuel Johnson into elegiac couplets. A paraphrase and notes based on the Rev. George Preston's solution are provided.*

> Evening now from purple wings
> Sheds the grateful gifts she brings;
> Brilliant drops bedeck the mead,
> Cooling breezes shake the reed,
> Shake the reed and curl the stream,
> Silvered o'er with Cynthia's beam;
> Near the chequered lonely grove
> Hears and keeps thy secrets, love.

Now from wings *colored*[1] with violet, evening *sprinkles*[2]
Whatever[3] gifts pleasing to the earth she brings back with her.
The fields decorated with shining gems flash,
A colder *breeze*[4] plays on the trembling reeds;[5]
It plays on the reeds and cools the fluvial waters
With a silvery light with which Cynthia *covers*[6] the *water.*[7]
There beneath the foliage the *quivering*[8] grove hears and conceals
Whatever you, *winged*[9] boy, do in secret.

---

* Adapted from *Exercises in Latin Verse*, p. 4.
[1] *tinctus*
[2] *irroro*
[3] *quot*
[4] place in the previous line.
[5] an unusual quinquesyllablic pentameter ending, but note the repetition at the start of the next line.
[6] *lino*
[7] *uadum*
[8] *coruscus*
[9] *ales*

EXERCISE XXXIVC

Translate Shakespeare's sonnet 54 into elegiac couplets. A paraphrase and notes based on the Rev. George Preston's solution are provided.*

O how much more doth beauty beauteous seem,
By that sweet ornament which truth doth give!
The rose looks fair, but fairer we it deem
For that sweet odour which doth in it live.
The canker blooms have full as deep a dye
As the perfumed tincture of the roses;
Hang on such thorns and play as wantonly
When summer's breath their masked buds discloses.
But, for their virtue only is their show,
They live unwoo'd and unrespected fade;
Die to themselves. Sweet roses do not so;
Of their sweet deaths are sweetest odours made;
And so of you, beauteous and lovely youth,
When that shall fade, my verse distills your truth.

A, how much more beautiful[1] beauty itself shines forth[2]
If only *glory*[3] *makes it worthwhile*[4] with *candor.*[5]
A certain rose is beautiful,[6] but *that which dwells within*[7] seems more beautiful
Because the pleasant odor of [its] husk[8] *is given off.*[9]
No less does the purple of rustic buds flash

* Adapted from *Exercises in Latin Verse*, p. 10.
[1] *formosior*
[2] *nito*
[3] *decus*
[4] *commendo*
[5] *simplicitas*
[6] *pulchra*
[7] *illa incola* (place "*incola*" in the next line)
[8] *calyx*
[9] *spiro* (active)

Than[10] *that*[11] wealthy color of *fragrant*[12] roses.
Thus the *hanging*[13] stamen bends and plays *wanton (games)*[14]
When the vernal North wind *opens up*[15] the enclosed *buds*.[16]
But indeed a *crimson*[17] *luster*[18] is for them [their] *only*[19] virtue,
[And] an *inglorious*[20] death brings to a close [their] *unadorned*[21] day.
Death *has snatched them all away.*[22] Not so the *sweet*[23] rose, but
Surviving[24] from a sweet death, a sweeter odor is *fragrant.*[25]
Thus to you, handsome boy, although that *charm*[26] falls away,
Our *muse*[27] *still*[28] *exhales*[29] your true glory.

[10] *quam* (postponed)
[11] *ipse*
[12] *odoriferus*
[13] *pensile*
[14] *lasciua*
[15] *resero*
[16] *germen*
[17] *puniceus*
[18] *nitor*
[19] *unicus*
[20] *inhonestus*
[21] *inornatus*
[22] *totus rapio*
[23] *suauis*
[24] *superstes*
[25] *halo* (place in the previous line)
[26] *ista uenustas*
[27] *Camena*
[28] *adhuc*
[29] *spiro*

SECTION X: THE SAPPHIC METER

The Sapphic meter takes its name from the Greek poet Sappho, who is tradition-ally credited with its invention. It was the second favorite lyric meter of Horace (used in twenty-five odes) and was used twice by Catullus, once by Statius, and occasionally by post-classical writers as well. The Sapphic stanza consists of three hendecasyllabic lines and one adonic. Its rhythmic pattern is schematized as follows:

$$- \cup - \breve{\cup} - \cup \cup - \cup - \breve{\cup}$$
$$- \cup - \breve{\cup} - \cup \cup - \cup - \breve{\cup}$$
$$- \cup - \breve{\cup} - \cup \cup - \cup - \breve{\cup}$$
$$- \cup \cup - \breve{\cup}$$

A Sapphic ode may have as many or as few stanzas as the poet desires,[1] but incomplete stanzas are not permitted.[2] The division of the hendecasyllables is the subject of some dispute, but they may usefully be thought of as two pairs of trochees surrounding a central dactyl. The second trochee in each pair may be replaced by a spondee at the discretion of the poet. A caesura divides the lines either after the fifth syllable (a "strong" caesura, $- \| \cup \cup$), e.g.,

$$- \cup - - - \; \| \; \cup \cup - \cup - -$$

iam satis terris // niuis atque dirae (Hor. *Carm.* 1.2.1)

or after the sixth (a "weak" caesura, $- \cup \| \cup$), e.g.,

$$- \cup - - - \cup \; \| \; \cup - \cup - -$$

flumen et regnata // petam Laconi (2.6.11).

In the first three books of Horace's *Odes*, the strong fifth-syllable caesura is by far the norm, but in book four the poet uses the sixth-syllable caesura with increasing

---

[1] Horace's shortest Sapphic in the *Odes* has two stanzas (1.38), and his longest consists of fifteen (4.2). The *Carmen Saeculare* is nineteen stanzas long.
[2] Lines are clearly missing from Catullus 51.

frequency.[3] It is also common in Catullus.[4] Because of the relative weakness of the sixth-syllable caesura, it is typically balanced by strong caesurae in both the second and fourth feet, e.g.,

$$- \cup - \| - - \cup \| \cup - \| \cup - \bar{\cup}$$

ille mi // par esse // deo // uidetur (Cat. 51.1), or

Mercuri // facunde // nepos // Atlantis (Hor. *Carm.* 1.10).

Catullus violates this principle only at 11.15, where the weak caesura is accompanied by a break in the fourth foot alone, and Horace strictly observes the rule in the first three books of the *Odes* but frequently disregards it in *Odes* 4 and the *Carmen Saeculare*.[5] A special effect may be intended in *feruet immensusque ruit profundo / Pindarus ore* (4.2.7–8) or in *pinus aut impulsa cupressus Euro* (4.6.10), where the lack of a strong break may suggest the rushing and unbroken tide of Pindaric song or the sweep of the East wind. Similarly, *'o Sol / pulcher! o laudande!' canam, recepto / Caesare felix* (47) cleverly juxtaposes the Sapphic meter with a septenarian rhythm.[6] On the other hand, there are many lines like *CS* 1 which seem to bear no special emphasis: *Phoebe siluarumque potens Diana.* Perhaps Horace simply decided to use a freer, more varied form in his later years, or perhaps he wanted to move closer to Greek practice. Nearly half of Sappho's verses either use a weak caesura or have no central break at all.[7] Accordingly, the sixth-syllable caesura is often found with a Greek word, e.g., *quem uirum aut heroa lyra uel acri* (1.12.1), or

---

[3] Nisbet and Hubbard I, xliv.

[4] The strong caesura is found in 60% of Catullus's lines, while the weak caesura occurs 27% of the time. 13% of Catullus's lines lack fifth- or sixth-syllable caesurae.

[5] With a weak third-foot caesura, Horace omits both the second- and the fourth-foot pauses in only three instances (4.2.38; *CS* 14, 59). When he includes just one compensatory pause, he shows a 2:1 preference for the second-foot caesura (4.2.9, 23, 33; 4.6.10; 4.11.23; *CS* 35, 58, 61, 73), but the fourth is also used by itself (4.2.7; *CS* 1, 54, 62). Postgate (mistakenly, to my mind) names the fourth-foot caesura as the normal alternative (*PL* 111), perhaps following the example of the hexameter. In the Sapphic, however, the second-foot pause is arguably the more pronounced since it not infrequently coincides with a sense break, e.g., 1.2.30, 1.25.6, 1.32.1, 2.8.5, 2.10.17, 3.14.10. I cannot find any similar stop after the eighth syllable. Indeed, if there is any recurring break near the end of the line, it is after the seventh syllable, e.g., 3.27.50ff. (*o deorum* ...!). Shall we call this the "Sapphic diaresis"?

[6] Heinze, *Die lyrischen Verse des Horaz*, Leipzig (1959). The trochaic septenarius is based on the following pattern: $- \cup / - - / - \cup / - - / - \cup / - - / - \cup / \bar{\cup}$. The portion in bold type above corresponds to feet 4–7. While the end of one hendecasyllable and the beginning of the next will always produce such a rhythm, the septenarian cadence is emphasized in this instance because the words in question are grouped together as a chant.

[7] The percentages are as follows: 53% (5th), 28% (6th), 19% (other).

a Greek name, e.g., *lenis, Ilithyia, tuere matres* (*CS* 14), and lines that lack a proper caesura may sometimes suggest a general "Greek" effect. In Catullus 11, for example, the poet uses irregular caesurae when he imagines Furius and Aurelius travelling in the East, but when the scene shifts to Italy, the more reliably Roman fifth-syllable caesura quickly asserts itself:

> seu Sagas sagittiferosue Parthos,
> siue quae septemgeminus colorat
>   aequora Nilus,
> siue trans altas gradietur Alpes,
> Caesaris uisens monimenta magni. . . (6–10).

In other instances, the absence of a fifth-syllable caesura may have no particular connection to the meaning of the line yet still serve the important poetic purpose of adding rhythmic variety to an ode. At 4.2.9, for instance, a weak caesura contributes to an impressively grand three-word line: *laurea donandus Apollinari.*

What, then, do these examples and statistics teach the modern versifier? If, for some reason, you want to imitate the Horace of *Odes* I–III, make a break after the fifth syllable most of the time, after the sixth rarely, and elsewhere only if some special effect is intended. Otherwise, treat the caesura a bit more casually: Make a break after the fifth syllable at least half of the time, after the sixth sometimes, and elsewhere occasionally, even if no special effect is intended.

ADDITIONAL CONSIDERATIONS

1) The Fourth Syllable: While a short fourth syllable is sometimes found in Catullus (e.g., 11.6 above) and the Greek poets, Horace always uses a long.

2) Elision: The rules of elision already learned apply to the lyric meters as well. Elision at the caesura is quite rare in the Sapphic meter (less so in the Alcaic), but it does occur and therefore need not be avoided entirely; however, a compensatory second-foot caesura is required, e.g., *imbrium // diuina auis imminentum* (3.27.10), and the second and fourth in combination is preferable, e.g., *Pegasus // terrenum equitem // grauatus* (4.11.27). Horace also writes lines such as *Thessalo uictore et ademptus Hector* (2.4.10) and *oderit curare et amara lento* (2.16.26), in which there is both elision at the strong caesura and a weak caesura after *et*.

3) Caesura: As in the hexameter, the Sapphic caesura will often coincide with a

sense break, e.g., *unde quo ueni? // leuis una mors est / uirginum culpae* (3.27.37–8), but not necessarily, e.g., *Poscimur. siquid // uacui sub umbra* (1.32.1). Similarly, it is not unusual to find the caesura after the word *et*, e.g., *o decus Phoebi et // dapibus supremi* (1.32.13). Lengthening of a natuarally short open vowel can occur only at the strong fifth-syllable caesura, and it is rare; the only example is 2.6.14, *angulus ridet ubi non Hymetto*.[8] Note that lyric caesurae, while important to the structure of a verse, were probably more lightly felt than those of the hexameter. Still, there is no line in any Latin Sapphic that has no caesura at all.

4) Hypermetric Lines: Although hypermetric lines are often attention-getting in the hexameter, they are somewhat less striking in the lyric meters, perhaps because the stanza, rather than the line, is the dominant metrical unit. Sometimes the hypermeter bears some special emphasis. In Catullus 11, the elision of *i* at the end of a line evokes the cutting of a flower on the edge of a meadow by a passing plow:

> qui illius culpa cecidit uelut prat(i)
> ultimi flos, praetereunte postquam
>   tactus aratro est (21–24).

Similarly, in Horace's lines,

> redditum Cyri solio Phraaten
> dissidens plebi numero beator(um)
> eximit Virtus (2.2.17–19),

the word *eximit* "takes out" the last syllable of *beatorum* just as Phraaten has been excluded from the number of the blessed. A similar effect may be present in the sixth stanza of 4.2:

> flebili sponsae iuuenemue raptum
> plorat et uires animumque moresqu(e)

---

[8] For the lengthening of -*et, at*, and -*it* (which may, at any rate, retain the trace of an older quantity) at the caesura in other meters, cf. 1.13.6, *certa sede manet umor et in genas*, and 3.16.26, *quam si quidquid arat impiger Apulus* (at Asclepiadic caesurae). More daringly, a syllable is lengthened in *arsis a) elsewhere in the Asclepiadic line, *perrupit Acheronta Herculeus labor* (1.3.36); b) in a Glyconic, *si figit adamantinos* (3.24.5); and c) in the fourth line of an Alcaic, *caeca timet aliunde fata* (2.13.16, for which see Nisbet and Hubbard *ad loc.* and v. 1, xliii).

    aureos educit in astra nigroqu(e)
    inuidet Orco (21–24).

Here, two successive interlinear elisions may represent a young hero's untimely death or the copious tears of his wife.[9] On the other hand, the hypermeter of *tibi tollit hinnit(um) / apta quadrigis equa* (2.16.4) seems to have no particular purpose, unless perhaps to suggest the speed of a race horse. In one instance, Horace even allows an elision between lines to attract the first syllable of the adonic to the end of the third hendecasyllable: *labitur ripa, Ioue non probant(e), ux- / orius amnis* (1.2.19–20). Indeed, the third and fourth lines of a Sapphic stanza share a particularly close linkage, and Sappho, who essentially treats them as a single line, often allows for word-sharing even when no elision is involved.[10] Although this license is less common in Horace than in his Greek models, its judicious use is not incompatible with classical Roman practice. Examples include *Thracio bacchante magis sub inter- / lunia uento* (1.25.11–12), and more daringly *Grosphe, non gemmis neque purpura ue- / nale neque auro* (2.16.7–8), as well as Catullus 11.11, where it is perhaps not too far-fetched to suggest that the division of *ulti-/ mosque Britannos* underscores the remoteness of the Britons.

5) Hiatus: Hiatus within a single line is largely confined to exclamations, where it is normal (e.g., *o utinam*), but hiatus between lines is more common than is often supposed. Indeed, the amount of misinformation in print on this topic is astonishing. The only hiatus Horace never allows is that of a short open vowel at the end of a hendecasyllable. Non-elision of a long vowel between hendecasyllables occurs eleven times,[11] and non-elision of an -*m* occurs three times.[12] Hiatus between the third hendecasyllable and the adonic is found in four instances, two involving a long vowel or diphthong[13] and two involving an -*m*.[14] Hiatus between stanzas is unremarkable (*synaloepha never occurs): non-elision of a

---

[9] Note, however, that the affected syllable in line 22 is the second -*que* in a -*que . . . -que* construction and therefore less unusual; cf. *CS* 47 and see p. 22 on the same phenomenon in the hexameter.

[10] The third stanza of the great hymn to Aphrodite is typical: πύκνα δίννεντες πτέρ' ἀπ' ὠράνωῦθε- / ρος διὰ μέσσω. Poem 16.3–4 is equally famous: ἔγω δὲ κῆν' ὄτ- / τω τις ἔραται.

[11] 1.2.6, 41; 1.12.6, 25; 1.25.18; 1.30.6; 2.2.6; 2.4.6; 2.16.5; 3.11.29, 50.

[12] 1.22.15, 3.27.33, and 3.27.10 (unless '*iminentium*' is read). See Nisbet and Hubbard (v. 1, xliv), who, although usually meticulous, have their totals wrong, for they acknowledge only 10 elisions between hendecasyllables.

[13] 1.12.7 and 31.

[14] 1.2.47 and 1.22.15.

long vowel in this position is found eleven times;[15] of a short, four times; and of an *-m*, four times.[16] While these statistics show that anxiety over hiatus in the Sapphic is largely misplaced, some restraint is nevertheless called for, and it should be noted that Horace prefers to make any interlinear hiatus correspond with a sense break whenever possible.

6) Enjambment: In order to achieve the maximum rhythmic variety within the relatively restrictive confines of the Sapphic meter, it is desirable to vary the position of sense breaks within a poem, as Horace does, and to allow sentences to extend not only from line to line but also from stanza to stanza. Although it is more typical than not for a Roman poet to end his stanzas at a sense break, enjambed stanzas are not so rare as verse teachers would have us believe, for a full 30% of Horace's stanzas end in mid-sentence.[17] Sometimes the enjambment is used to good effect, e.g., (2.8.4–5), where *crederem* is the emphatic apodosis to three *si* clauses,[18] or 1.2.49, where the enjambment of *tollat* suggests the force of a sudden breeze, or 2.10.17, where *idem / summouet* forms a nice antithesis with *reducit* as Jupiter both brings hideous winters and takes them away. In other cases, enjambment may simply be a way to prevent rhythmic monotony from setting in.[19] The avoidance of enjambment may be equally purposeful, and the adonic, which reminds one of a hexameter ending, can serve as an effective cap to a stanza, e.g., *risit Apollo* (1.10.12), or an entire poem, e.g., *te duce, Caesar* (1.2.52), *uatis amici* (2.6.24), and the appropriately final *perdidit urbes* (Cat. 51.16); also effective is the little jingle that both closes a stanza and echoes the ebb and flow of a wave in Catullus's *tunditur unda* (11.4) and Horace's *unda recumbit* (1.12.32). In addition, Horace sometimes likes to connect stanzas by repeating a word or phrase from the Adonic in the next hendecasyllable, e.g., *terruit urbem / terruit gentis* (1.2.4–5); *mouit Achillem / mouit Aiacem* (2.4.4–5); and, more subtly,

> . . . quorum simul alba nautis

---

[15] 1.2.16; 1.12.4, 8; 2.6.12; 2.8.12; 3.8.8; 3.11.32; 3.14.4; 3.20.8; 4.6.12; *CS* 60.

[16] 1.12.40, 2.6.8, 2.8.8, 3.27.36 and 1.32.12, 2.10.4, 2.16.28, 4.11.12 respectively. Verrall 180 misses 2.10.4 and Lupton xxvii misinterprets his statistic to refer to all line endings rather than stanza endings.

[17] Wilkinson 106 offers the statistic of 62 out of 204.

[18] See Nisbet and Hubbard *ad loc.*

[19] One might profitably contrast Horace's practice with that of Statius, for whom the stanza is almost always a complete unit of thought. Such tightness of form is, of course, a valid aesthetic principle, but it also deprives the poem of musical variety, especially since Statius couples the lack of enjambment with an unwavering use of the strong caesura.

> stella refulsit,
> defluit saxis agitatus umor (1.12.27–29),

in which *refulsit* and *defluit* are elegantly juxtaposed to show how the water flows down from the rocks "just as soon as" the star shines forth.

7) More on the Adonic: The position of word-breaks in the adonic closely follows those of the fifth and sixth feet of the hexameter. The most common patterns are *uisere montes* ($-\cup\cup \mid -\overset{\smile}{-}$) and *augur Apollo* ($-\cup \mid \cup-\overset{\smile}{-}$), but *gratus et imis* ($-\cup \mid \cup \mid -\overset{\smile}{-}$) and *cum lare fundus* ($- \mid \cup\cup \mid -\overset{\smile}{-}$) also occur rather frequently. A one-word Adonic occurs just four times,[20] and a quadrisyllabic ending occurs only once: *seu Genitalis* (*CS* 16). A monosyllabic ending is equally rare, occurring only at 4.11.4: *est hederae uis*. In the hexameter, such an ending often conveys sudden force, a sense that is well-suited to the monosyllable "*uis*," yet there may be less here than meets the eye since Horace is simply describing the "large supply of ivy" to be used as a garland.

---

[20] 1.12.40, 1.30.8, 2.6.8, and 4.11.28.

EXERCISE XXXV: SAPPHIC SCANSION

Scan the following Horatian ode (1.12), marking caesurae and noting elisions
when they occur. Other subtleties of versification such as hiatus between lines,
word order, and the position of sense breaks within and between stanzas should
also be observed.

Quem uirum aut heroa lyra uel acri
tibia sumis celebrare, Clio?
quem deum? cuius recinet iocosa
    nomen imago

aut in umbrosis Heliconis oris
aut super Pindo gelidoue in Haemo,
unde uocalem temere insecutae
    Orphea siluae

arte materna rapidos morantem
fluminum lapsus celerisque uentos,
blandum et auritas fidibus canoris
    ducere quercus?

quid prius dicam solitis parentis
laudibus, qui res hominum ac deorum,
qui mare ac terras uariisque mundum
    temperat horis?

unde nil maius generatur ipso,
nec uiget quicquam simile aut secundum:
proximos illi tamen occupabit
    Pallas honores.

proeliis audax, neque te silebo,
Liber, et saeuis inimica Virgo
beluis, nec te, metuende certa
    Phoebe sagitta.

dicam et Alciden puerosque Ledae,
hunc equis, illum superare pugnis
nobilem; quorum simul alba nautis
    stella refulsit,

defluit saxis agitatus umor,
concidunt uenti fugiuntque nubes,
et minax, quod sic uoluere, ponto
    unda recumbit.

Romulum post hos prius an quietum
Pompili regnum memorem an superbos
Tarquini fasces, dubito, an Catonis
    nobile letum.

Regulum et Scauros animaeque magnae
prodigum Paulum superante Poeno
gratus insigni referam Camena
    Fabriciumque.

hunc et incomptis Curium capillis
utilem bello tulit et Camillum
saeua paupertas et auitus apto
    cum lare fundus.

crescit occulto uelut arbor aeuo
fama Marcelli; micat inter omnis
Iulium sidus, uelut inter ignis
    luna minores.

gentis humanae pater atque custos,
orte Saturno, tibi cura magni
Caesaris fatis data: tu secundo
    Caesare regnes.

ille seu Parthos Latio imminentis
egerit iusto domitos triumpho,
siue subiectos Orientis orae
    Seras et Indos,

te minor laetum reget aequus orbem:
tu graui curru quaties Olympum,
tu parum castis inimica mittes
fulmina lucis.

EXERCISE XXXVI: JUMBLED SAPPHIC HENDECASYLLABLES

Rearrange the following groups of words so that each will stand as a proper Sapphic hendecasyllabic line. There are no elisions in lines 1–15, but lines 16–20 each contain at least one elision. A weak caesura is required in lines 2, 3, 6, and 18.

1. carmen Maximo tempto tenuare

2. timet Medus Albanasque secures

3. equo Mineruae non ille inclusus

4. sed puer ante artes tuas discat

5. fidicen doctor Thaliae argutae

6. decus Dauniae Camenae defende

7. Priamus diues Ilio relicto

8. arbor aura aestiua recreatur

9. albescens capillus animos lenit

10. lupus inter agnos audaces errat

11. silua tibi frondes agrestes spargit

12. quatiunt parcius fenestras iunctas

13. uisens monimenta Caesaris magni

14. hic pater atque princeps dici ames

15. mors cita clarum Achillem abstulit

16. ego calidus iuuenta non ferrem hoc

17. Faune, amator fugientum Nympharum

18. nec meum amorem respectet, ut ante

19. exsultas otio gestis -que nimium

20. non arcu neque Mauris iaculis eget

EXERCISE XXXVII: THE SAPPHIC STANZA

Translate each of the following English phrases and sentences into Latin Sapphic verse. Numbers 1–5 are single hendecasyllabic lines, 6–8 are entire stanzas in which the line breaks have been identified for you, and 9–10 are stanzas without any specified line divisions.

1. without you there is sluggishness for my muse (pl.)
   sine tu Camenae nostrae torpor sum

2. now the bands powerful on land and sea . . .
   iam manus potens mare terra -que

3. now for a long time satisfied by the wide field . . .
   satiata iam diu campus latus

4. go (sing.) where your feet and the breezes carry you
   eo quo pedes et aurae tu rapio

5. in the midst of triumph, Atrides burned
   in medius triumphus Atrides ardeo

6. The whole band is hurrying; here and there
   girls mixed with boys rush.
   The flames tremble as they roll dirty
   smoke in a whirlwind.

   manus cuncta festino, huc et illuc
   puellae mixtae pueri cursito;
   trepido flammae rotans sordidus
   fumus uertex.

7. Gentle and calm with your weapon concealed,
   Apollo, hear the suppliant boys;

Two-horned queen of the stars, hear
the girls, Luna.

mitis placidus -que conditum telum
Apollo audio supplices pueri;
audio regina bicornis sidus
Luna puellae.

8. Tigers and the accompanying woods you are able
   to lead and to delay the swift rivers;
   to you, the charming one, yields the monstrous
   doorman of the hall (of Hades).

   tigres comitesque siluae tu possum
   duco et moror riui celeres;
   tu blandiens cedo immanis
   ianitor aula.

9. May the earth, fertile in crops and cattle, present Ceres
   with a crown of corn, and may both the healthful rains and the
   breezes of Jove nourish the crops.

   tellus fertilis frux pecusque Ceres spicea corona dono;
   et aqua salubris et aura Iouis fetus nutrio.

10. And you, Pindar, ruler of the lyric band, give me the
    jurisdiction (pl.) of a new lyre for a while if I have made
    your Thebes sacred with Latin song.

    tuque Pindar regnator lyrica cohors do ego iura nouum plectrum
    paulum si sacro tuae Thebae cantus Latius.

EXERCISE XXXVIIIA: SAPPHICS
FROM A PARAPHRASE

Translate the following lines from Herrick into a Latin Sapphic stanza. A paraphrase adapted from J. H. Lupton's *Latin Lyric Verse Composition* is provided.

> While fates permit us, let us be merry;
> Pass all we must the fatal ferry;
> And this our life too whirls away
> With the rotation of the day.

> While *it is allowed*[1] to us, let us jest *merrily;*[2]
> The *fords*[3] of *Death*[4] must be crossed by all;
> Life *whirls on*[5] as the *daily*[6]
> Orbit revolves.

[1] *licet*

[2] *hilares*

[3] *uada*

[4] Since both *Mortis* and *Leti* will scan, the composer is left with a stylistic choice. While Horace personifies death as *Mors* at 1.4.13, a poem with a similar theme, *Letum* is perhaps to be preferred for its grandeur and because *omnibus Leti* sounds better than the pointlessly sibilant *omnibus Mortis*.

[5] *torquetur*

[6] *diurna*

EXERCISE XXXVIIIB

Translate the following lines from Dryden into Sapphic stanzas. A paraphrase is again provided.*

The praise of Bacchus then the sweet musician sung,
Of Bacchus ever fair and ever young;
    The jolly god in triumph comes,
    Sound the trumpets, beat the drums!
    Flushed with a purple grace
    He shows his honest face;
Now give the hautboys breath; he comes, he comes!

Bacchus, ever fair and young,
    Drinking joys did first ordain;
Bacchus' blessings are a treasure,
Drinking is the soldier's pleasure:
    Rich the treasure,
    Sweet the pleasure;
Sweet is pleasure after pain.

Then in sweet praise and *rhythms*,[1] the poet
sings the glory of Bacchus. Ever handsome,
behold, Bacchus *is vigorous*[2] in the *primal*[3]
flower of *youth*.[4]

Now the god comes in a happy triumph;
Let the trumpets give voice, let the drums'

---

  * This poem is also adapted from Lupton; however, some of the lines have been altered either for the sake of clarity or to achieve greater adherence to the sense of the Dryden poem.

  [1] *numeri*

  [2] *uigeo*

  [3] *primaeuus*

  [4] *iuuenta*

new force thunder *on all sides.*[5] Ruddiness and *beauty*[6]
mark[7] the honorable

face[8] of the god. Now, now, fill the *reeds*[9]
with breath: Bacchus comes, ever handsome;
He comes always *rejoicing*[10] in the primal
flower of youth.

Who *before*[11] Bacchus *is said*[12] *to have laid down*[13]
the pacts and *merry*[14] laws of *drinking?*[15]
Thus does the *treasure*[16] grow well. The *soldier*[17]
an ample pleasure

from this source[18] makes *happy:*[19] surely it is a rich treasure.
Surely there is sweet pleasure in *wine.*[20]
A sweet *pleasure rightly*[21] follows pain *when driven away.*[22]

[5] *passim*
[6] *uenustas*
[7] *signo*
[8] *os*
[9] *calami*
[10] *exsultans*
[11] *prior* + ablative
[12] *fertur*
[13] *pono* – note that the perfect infinitive is needed
[14] *hilares*
[15] *bibo* (gerund)
[16] *gaza*
[17] The accusative is needed here; use "*militantem.*"
[18] *hinc*
[19] *beo*
[20] Use "*Bromius*" (in the dative), another name for Bacchus.
[21] These two words should be placed in the final line.
[22] *exactum*

SECTION XI: THE ALCAIC METER

The Alcaic meter is named for the Greek poet Alcaeus, who is traditionally credited with its invention. It is Horace's favorite lyric meter (used in thirty-seven odes) but is used only once by Statius. Accordingly, the guidelines and exercises that follow are based chiefly on Horatian usage. The Alcaic stanza consists of two "Greater Alcaic" hendecasyllabic lines followed by a trochaic dimeter with *anacrusis (nine syllables) and a "Minor Alcaic" (ten syllables). The stanza's rhythmic pattern is schematized as follows.

Although Alcaeus commonly uses an initial short syllable in any of his first three lines, Horace prefers a long, e.g., *aequam memento rebus in arduis* (2.3.1), but occasionally substitutes a short, e.g., *uides ut alta stet niue candidum* (1.9.1).[1] Similarly, whereas Alcaeus sometimes allows a short fifth syllable in the hendecasyllables, Horace invariably uses a long.[2]

Although Greek Alcaics lack a fixed caesura, the hendecasyllables of the Latin Alcaic are almost always divided by a strong caesura following the fifth syllable.

$$\breve{} \quad - \quad \cup \quad - \quad - \quad \| \quad - \quad \cup \quad \cup \quad - \quad \cup \quad \bar{\cup}$$

Velox amoenum ‖ *saepe Lucretilem*

This caesura is less flexible than that of the Sapphic hendecasyllable, and exceptions are quite rare.[3] When they do occur, special significance is sometimes felt. The famous Cleopatra ode (1.37) provides a particularly effective example:

---

[1] L. J. Richardson (1907) 203–4 identifies just twenty-nine such cases: nineteen in lines one and two, and ten in line three. That amounts to only 3% of a possible 951 lines.

[2] There is one possible exception: *si non periret immiserabilis* (3.5.17), but Nisbet and Hubbard v.1 xli rightly consider this to be a case of irregular lengthening at the caesura rather than a true short syllable.

[3] There are only five instances in Horace: 1.16.21, 1.37.5, 1.37.14, 2.17.21, and 4.14.17.

> ... sed minuit furorem
> uix una sospes nauis ab ignibus,
> mentemque lymphatam Mareotico
> redigit in ueros timores
> Caesar ... (12–16).

Here the absence of a caesura gives line 14 an irregular rhythm perhaps suggestive of Cleopatra's drunken frenzy as she is pursued by Octavian. It may also ironically reflect the poet's own intoxication as he celebrates the queen's defeat. Indeed, in his enthusiasm to bring forth the Caecuban wine, Horace had already run over the caesura in line five: *antehac nefas depromere Caecubum.* Similarly, in poem 1.16, an *insolens exercitus* plows through the caesura, giving the line an unrestrained rhythm that nicely complements the poet's warnings about the dangers of unrestrained anger:

> ... cur perirent
> funditus imprimeretque muris
> hostile aratrum exercitus insolens (19–21).

Elision at the caesura: Elision at the caesura occurs when the elided syllable falls before the caesura, e.g., *mentem sacerdot(um) // incola Pythius.* While this phenomenon is relatively rare in the Sapphic, it is not so uncommon in the Alcaic: There are twenty-four instances in *Odes* 1–3 but none in the four Alcaics of book four. In two cases Horace daringly elides two syllables in synizesis before the caesura: *uos lene consil(ium) // et datis et dato* (3.4.41) and *hinc omne princip(ium) // huc refer exitum* (3.6.6). Although the synizesis is not, in itself, unprecedented,[4] I am aware of no instances in any other meter in which it is combined with an elision at the caesura.

Hypermetric lines: Hypermetric lines are rare in the Horatian Alcaic. There are only two instances, and both occur between the third and fourth lines. In each case the elision arguably carries some special force. *Odes* 2.3 ends with a reminder that we are all fated to die. In the poem's final lines, the *exilium* imposed by Fate takes away the final syllable of *aeternum* just as we will be taken away from life:

> omnes eodem cogimur, omnium

---

[4] For a general discussion of synizesis, see Part I. In the Alcaic meter, other examples include *Prometheus* (1.16.13, 2.13.37), *anteit* (1.35.17), *antehac* (1.37.5), *Pompei* (2.7.5), and *Typhoeus* (3.4.53).

> uersatur urna serius ocius
> sors exitura et nos in aetern(um)
> exsilium impositura cumbae (25–28).

This elision, together with *exitur(a) et* and *exsili(um) impositura*, also gives the lines a flowing and unbroken rhythm perhaps indicative of the undulations of the Styx. Such a reading is supported by 3.29.35–36 in which an interlinear elision may be imitative of a river's seamless flow into the sea:

> cum pace delabentis Etrusc(um)
> in mare, nunc lapides adesos. . . .

Hiatus: The observations made about hiatus in the Sapphic meter are largely applicable for the Alcaic as well. Within a line, hiatus is confined to exclamations. Between lines it is rare but not so rare as to be avoided entirely.[5] The least common hiatus is that of a short vowel at the end of a hendecasyllable (which occurs only at 1.17.3–4), and the hiatus of a short vowel between lines 3 and 4 occurs only twice (1.16.27 and 2.13.7).

FINER POINTS

Lines 1 and 2: There is little agreement concerning the proper foot divisions of the hendecasyllables, but L. J. Richardson makes a convincing case for classifying the lines as Epionic Trimeters Catalectic:

$$\overset{\smile}{-} \; - \; \smile \; - \; | \; - \; - \; \smile \; \smile \; | \; - \; \smile \; \overset{\smile}{-}$$

When we recall the principle that word and foot divisions seldom correspond in the first part of a line but often correspond at the end, Richardson's formulation successfully accounts for Horace's favorite patterns. The first hemistich usually consists of two words, most commonly following the model of *odi profanum* ($- - | \smile - -$) or *descende caelo* ($- - \smile | - -$), but occasionally *me fabulosae* ($- | - \smile - -$). When three words are used, Horace prefers to begin with a monosyllable, e.g., *o matre pulchra* ($- | - \smile | - -$) or *cur me querellis* ($- | - | \smile - -$). On occasion the poet allows a single word to take him to the caesura, e.g., *fastidiosus* ($- - \smile - \overset{\smile}{-}$). Only rarely will the hemistich end with a monosyllable, and in such cases, that monosyllable will usually

---

[5] There are 50 cases out of approximetely 1200 opportunities in Horace, or 4%.

be preceded by another, e.g., *Soracte, nec iam*. The violation of this principle, how-ever, can sometimes add emphasis to a line, as in 2.17,

>   a, te meae si partem animae rapit
>   maturior uis . . . (5–6),

where the monosyllable *uis* represents the forceful blow of fate that Horace fears may snatch Maecenas from him.[6] In the second hemistich, Horace shows a strong preference for ending the line with a word of three syllables, preceded either by another trisyllable, e.g., *latius ordinet* (– ∪ ∪ | – ∪ ≍), or a monosyllable and disyllable in combination, e.g., *ac sine funibus* (– | ∪ ∪ | – ∪ ≍) or *uulgus et arceo* (– ∪ | ∪ | – ∪ ≍). A disyllabic line ending is also frequently used, e.g., *ter crepuit sonum* (– | ∪ ∪ – | ∪ ≍), *Mercurius celer* (– ∪ ∪ – | ∪ ≍), and *carmina non prius* (– ∪ ∪ | – | ∪ ≍), and double disyllabic endings, e.g., *census erat breuis* (– ∪ | ∪ – | ∪ ≍), are not as rare as is commonly supposed.[7] Line endings of four or five syllables are possible as well, and they can add some variety to the rhythm, e.g., *templa refeceris* (– ∪ | ∪ – ∪ ≍) and *hic generosior* (– | ∪ ∪ – ∪ ≍). Only rarely will a single word occupy the entire second hemistich, but its judicious use can be very effective, as in *Odes* 3.5.17f.:

>   si non periret immiserabilis
>   captiua pubes . . . .

Here, the line ending *immiserabilis* contributes to the sense of gravity and pathos that pervades this ode about bravery and sacrifice in war. In the same poem, a two-word hendecasyllable, *dissentientis condicionibus* (14), gives a similarly appropri-ate weight and dignity to the deeds of Regulus. Horace also generally avoids ending a line with a monosyllable, even if it is involved in an elision. Without an elision, there are only two examples in the hendecasyllables:

>   cur non sub alta uel platano, uel hac (2.11.13)
>   ne forte credas interitura, quae (4.9.1).

Line 3: The third line of the Alcaic stanza can be challenging to produce, and

---

[6] One finds a similar use of *uis* at the end of Vergilian hexameters, e.g., the Ennian-sounding *Aen.* 9.532 (*summaque euertere opum ui*) and 12.552 (*summa nituntur opum ui*); cf. also 4.132, 10.864, and 11.373.

[7] Anthon 226 writes that "it is better not to end this verse with two disyllables." His caution is well taken, but the ending need not be avoided entirely since Horace uses it thirty-one times or just under 5% of a possible 634 lines.

Anthon justifiably advises that the best way to acquire "an ear for the rhythm" is by reading Horace (227). The poet's most common pattern follows the model of *ornare puluinar deorum* ($- - \cup | - - - | \cup - \times$), i.e. three words of three syllables each. Furthermore, Horace favors a trisyllabic ending even when it is preceded by other combinations, e.g., *te praeter inuisas cupressos* ($- | - \cup | - - - | \cup - \times$), *frustra per autumnos nocentem* ($- - | \cup | - - - | \cup - \times$), *tinguet pauimentum superbo* ($- - | \cup - - - | \cup - \times$), *uenator in campis niualis* ($- - \cup | - | - - | \cup - \times$), and *excepit ictus pro pudicis* ($- - \cup | - - | - | \cup - \times$). In the last two examples, a trisyllabic beginning is used in combination with a trisyllabic ending, but a word of three syllables will also start lines in which a disyllabic ending is used, e.g., *monstrumue submisere Colchi* ($- - \cup | - - - \cup | - \times$). Several other patterns are possible as well, but the seven models given above should be followed most of the time, and the modern versifier would do well to refrain from using any pattern that does not have an exact parallel in Horace. Monosyllabic line endings are rare, and Horace has only one such example in the third line, *depone sub lauru mea, nec* (2.7.19), where Nisbet and Hubbard may be right to suggest that "the slumping rhythm seems to hint at weariness" (2.118). In addition, quadrisyllabic endings were considered inelegant, perhaps even barbarous or viperish, e.g.,

> regumque matres barbarorum et (1.35.11)
> nodo coerces uiperino (2.19.19),

and in *Odes* 2.3, *ab insolenti temperatum / laetitia* (3–4) may reflect an ironic *lack* of restraint from excessive joy.

Line 4: In the fourth line there is often a word break after the fourth syllable. A quadrisyllabic word provides an elegant opening and is frequently used by Horace, e.g., *Hesperiae* ($- \cup \cup -$), but a monosyllable and trisyllable, e.g., *nec ueteres* ($- | \cup \cup -$), or two disyllables, e.g., *sperne puer* ($- \cup | \cup -$), are also common. On the other hand, a disyllable followed by either a monosyllable, e.g., *funus et* ($- \cup | \cup$), or a polysyllabic word, e.g., *cuncta supercilio* ($- \cup | \cup - \cup \cup -$), are comparatively rare but nonetheless legitimate line openings. Furthermore, there is no prohibition against beginning the line with a self-contained dactyl, and Horace often follows the model of *flumina constiterint acuto* ($- \cup \cup | - \cup \cup - | \cup - -$). The minor Alcaic almost always ends with a word of either two or three syllables, but a six-syllable word can add grandeur to two-word lines like *diuitias operosiores* ($- \cup \cup - | \cup \cup - \cup - -$).

On the Strophe as a Whole: Because the Alcaic is a strophic meter, the end of a sentence will often correspond with the end of a strophe, but Horace by no means restricts himself to this practice. Other common places for a sense break are at the end of any line, after the third syllable of the hendecasyllables, or at the caesura of the hendecasyllables. A full stop anywhere in the third or fourth lines is quite rare,[8] and several exceptions to this rule are remarkable. In 1.35, an unusual sequence of sentence endings seems to underscore the poet's frustration and shame at the wickedness of civil war:

> eheu, cicatricum et sceleris pudet
> fratrumque. quid nos dura refugimus
>   aetas? quid intactum nefasti
>   liquimus? unde manum iuuentus
> metu deorum continuit? (33–37).

More subtly, a rare sense break in the third line (especially when combined with a rare double disyllabic ending) perhaps evokes the fear and excitement of Bacchic possession:

> euhoe, recenti mens trepidat metu,
> plenoque Bacchi pectore turbidum
>   laetatur. euhoe, parce, Liber,
>   parce, graui metuende thyrso (2.19.5–8).

In 4.15, when a sound from Apollo's lyre cuts short Horace's attempt at an epic, the poet abruptly shifts to an ode in praise of Augustus:

> Phoebus uolentem proelia me loqui
> uictas et urbes increpuit lyra,
>   ne parua Tyrrhenum per aequor
>   uela darem. tua, Caesar, aetas . . . (1–4).

Here, a strong sense break in the fourth line heightens the sense of Apollo's intrusiveness and Horace's sudden turn to a new subject. In two other instances the poet makes a break in the fourth line after an opening dactyl in order to introduce a contrasting point (2.13.8 and 2.17.8). And as in the hexameter, a single dactylic enjambed word can suggest violent or sudden action:

> quo bruta tellus et uaga flumina

---

[8] Conceding that what counts as a "full stop" is a somewhat problematic thing to determine, I can identify only seven cases: 1.34.12, 1.35.35, 2.3.11, 2.13.8, 2.17.8, 2.19.7, and 4.15.4.

> quo Styx et inuisi horrida Taenari
> sedes Atalanteusque finis
> concutitur (1.34.9–12).

Such variation of syntactic units within and across the strophic structures of the Alcaic is an artistic principle which the modern composer would do well to emulate.

EXERCISE XXXIX: ALCAIC SCANSION

Scan the following Horatian ode (4.14), marking caesurae and noting elisions when they occur. Other subtleties of versification such as hiatus between lines, word order, and the position of sense-breaks within and between stanzas should also be observed.

> Quae cura patrum quaeue Quiritium
> plenis honorum muneribus tuas,
>   Auguste, uirtutes in aeuum
>   per titulos memoresque fastus
>
> aeternet, o qua sol habitabilis
> illustrat oras, maxime principum?
>   quem legis expertes Latinae
>   Vindelici didicere nuper
>
> quid Marte posses. milite nam tuo
> Drusus Genaunos, implacidum genus,
>   Breunosque ueloces et arces
>   Alpibus impositas tremendis
>
> deiecit acer plus uice simplici;
> maior Neronum mox graue proelium
>   commisit immanisque Raetos
>   auspiciis pepulit secundis,
>
> spectandus in certamine Martio,
> deuota morti pectora liberae
>   quantis fatigaret ruinis,
>   indomitas prope qualis undas
>
> exercet Auster Pleiadum choro
> scindente nubes, impiger hostium
>   uexare turmas et frementem
>   mittere equum medios per ignis.

sic tauriformis uoluitur Aufidus,
qui regna Dauni praefluit Apuli,
    cum saeuit horrendamque cultis
        diluuiem meditatur agris,

ut barbarorum Claudius agmina
ferrata uasto diruit impetu
    primosque et extremos metendo
        strauit humum sine clade uictor,

te copias, te consilium et tuos
praebente diuos. nam tibi quo die
    portus Alexandrea supplex
        et uacuam patefecit aulam,

fortuna lustro prospera tertio
belli secundos reddidit exitus,
    laudemque et optatum peractis
        imperiis decus arrogauit.

te Cantaber non ante domabilis
Medusque et Indus, te profugus Scythes
    miratur, o tutela praesens
        Italiae dominaeque Romae.

te, fontium qui celat origines,
Nilusque et Hister, te rapidus Tigris,
    te beluosus qui remotis
        obstrepit Oceanus Britannis,

te non pauentis funera Galliae
duraeque tellus audit Hiberiae,
    te caede gaudentes Sygambri
        compositis uenerantur armis.

EXERCISE XL: JUMBLED ALCAIC LINES

Unscramble the following lines of an Alcaic strophe. Numbers 1–10 are hendecasyllables (lines one and two), numbers 11–15 are enneasyllables (line three), and numbers 16–20 are decasyllables (line four). Items marked with an asterisk contain an elision.

1. grandine non uerberatae uineae
2. pisces aequora contracta sentiunt
3. atrium sublime ritu moliar
4. et mors uirum fugacem persequitur
5. hospes famosus nec domus Priami
6. hoc lyrae iocosae non conueniet
7. Britannos feros hospitibus uisam
8. propositi uirum tenacem et iustum*
9. consiliantibus gratum elocuta*
10. qui mare qui inertem terram temperat*
11. turmas diuosque mortalesque
12. Orion temptator Dianae
13. dederunt multa di neglecti
14. tempestas ab Euro demissa
15. saporem dulcem elaborabunt*
16. balanus pressa capillis tuis
17. quod semel hora fugiens uexit
18. nisus insolitos docuere
19. Romae fumum et opes strepitumque*
20. sollicitam frontem explicuere

EXERCISE XLI: THE ALCAIC STANZA

Translate the following phrases and sentences to form lines of an Alcaic strophe. Numbers 1–6 are hendecasyllables (lines one and two), numbers 3–9 are enneasyllables (line three), and numbers 10–12 are decasyllables (line four). Number 13 represents lines one and two together, and number 14 represents lines three and four.

1. o daughter fairer than your fair mother
   o filia pulchrior mater pulchra

2. trained to shoot Seric arrows
   doctus tendo Sericae sagittae

3. for them the private estate was small
   illi census priuatus breuis sum

4. they have calmed the winds on the seething main
   sterno uenti aequor feruidus

5. dividing the clouds with flashing fire
   diuidens nubila ignis coruscus

6. and we see Aeacus the judge
   et Aeacus iudicans uideo

7. beneath a pleasant grotto, Pyrrha
   sub antrum gratum Pyrrha

8. to consecrate him with a Lesbian lyre
   Lesbium plectrum hic sacro

9. Autumn will paint the clusters (of grapes)
   Autumnus racemi distinguo

10. garments for the god of the sea
    uestimenta deus mare

11. nor do they fear green snakes
    nec colubrae uirides metuo

12. to seek rhythms with a lighter plectrum
    quaero modi plectrum leuior

13. I seem to hear great leaders soiled with not inglorious dust
    uideo audio duces magni sordidi puluis non indecorus

14. for whom the laurel won eternal honors in a Dalmatian triumph
    qui laurus aeterni honores pario triumphum Delmaticum

EXERCISE XLIIA: ALCAICS
FROM A PARAPHRASE

Translate the following lines from Dryden into Latin Alcaic stanzas. A paraphrase adapted from J. H. Lupton's *Latin Lyric Verse Composition* is provided.

Fairest isle, all isles excelling,
    Seat of pleasures and of loves;
Venus here will choose her dwelling,
    And forsake her Cyprian groves.

Cupid from his favourite nation
    Care and envy will remove;
Jealousy that poisons passion
    And despair that dies for love.

Gentle murmurs, sweet complaining,
    Sighs that blow the fire of love;
Soft repulses, kind disdaining,
    Shall be all the pains you prove.

O isle, loveable beyond all,
    the seat of loves and gladness,
shady *Cyprus*[1] on account of you will *Venus*[2]
    forsake, but from *his own*[3] (people) will Cupid

take away *all bitterness and envy,*[4]
    that none by *jealousy,*[5] none by lovers'

---

[1] Note that Cyprus is feminine and should be placed in the previous line.
[2] Use "Dione" for Venus.
[3] *proprii*
[4] Lit. "whatever of bitter and of envious," i.e. use *quodcumque* plus the genitive of the adjectives *amarus* and *inuidus*.
[5] *liuor*

hope *deluded,*[6] and *hating the light,*[7]
   may die.[8] For you the only care is

sweet complaints, gentle murmurs,
   sighs[9] *fanning*[10] the flames of the heart,
and the *endearments*[11] of soft disdain and repulse
   soon yielding.[12]

[6] *falsus*
[7] Lit. "hateful toward the light," i.e. *perosus* plus the accusative of respect.
[8] Remember that a compound verb may be substituted for a simple form.
[9] *lamenta*
[10] Use the present participle of *alo* and try to achieve an artful arrangement of words in this line.
[11] *blanditiae*, which should be placed in the next line
[12] When an adjective is metrically uncooperative, the poets commonly use *non* or *male* plus its opposite.

EXERCISE XLIIB

Translate the following lines from Meredith into Latin Alcaic stanzas. A paraphrase adapted from the Rev. George Preston's *Exercises in Latin Verse* is provided. Note that hyperbaton sometimes renders a line-by-line paraphrase impossible. When this occurs, the affected clause or sentence is underlined.

> Only the heaven is high,
> Only the gods are great
> Above the searchless sky,
> In unremoved state.
> They from their golden mansions
> Look over the lands and seas,
> The Ocean's wide expansions
> And the Earth's varieties;
> Secure of their supremecy,
> And sure of affluent ease.
> Who shall say "I stand" nor fall?
> Destiny is over all.
> Rust will crumble old renown,
> Bust and column tumble down,
> Keep and castle, tower and town,
> Throne and scepter, crest and crown.
> Destiny is over all!
> One by one the pale guests fall
> At lighted feast in palace hall
> And feast is turned to funeral.
> Who shall say "I stand" nor fall?
> Destiny is over all!

> The gods stand *on high*;[1] the singular glory
> Of an *unrivaled*[2] name they boast,
> The gods fierce in unchanging affaris
> Above the undiscovered fortress of the *sky*.[3]

---

[1] *in supremo*
[2] use *non* + the gerundive
[3] *polum*

They, reclining in golden *shrines*[4],
The waves and breezes and various *conditions*[5]
Of the Earth and the vast *space*[6]
Of the *outstretched*[7] Ocean they survey.

But Faith, *secure*[8] in wielding power
And *relaxing*[9] luxuriously
Calms all things. Who on high
Clouds, unafraid of ruin,

Will lift himself up? Certain Necessity
Presses upon all[10], Old Age will tear down
Its ancient name[11] and will strike down
The column bound with images of our ancestors.

The palace does not stand in the way of time, no less
the turreted structure, not the diadem,
Not the scepter, not the fasces, but with equal
Power[12] the Fates press upon all things.

Although the festive hall may shine
With lamps, a pale *guest*[13] strikes a falling
Guest, and the feasts
Libitina overturns with funerals.

---

[4] *aedes*
[5] *uices*
[6] place in the next line
[7] place in the previous line
[8] *secura* + genitive
[9] *feriata*
[10] place in the previous line
[11] place in the previous line
[12] Preston's solution requires the verb *ditio*, which is non-classical and therefore best avoided in original verse.
[13] *conuiua* (m.), place in the next line

EXERCISE XLIIc

The following exercise was used to determine the Merton, New, Magdalen, Corpus, and Worcester College scholarships at Oxford in 1891: Translate Thomas Campion's "Hymn in Praise of Neptune"[1] into Latin Alcaics. A paraphrase of the Rev. Dr. William Baker's solution is provided, although students competing at Oxford over a century ago received no such assistance.

Of Neptune's empire let us sing,
At whose command the waves obey;
To whom the rivers tribute pay,
Down the high mountains sliding:[2]
To whom the scaly nation yields
Homage for the crystal fields
    Wherein they dwell:
And every sea-dog[3] pays a gem
Yearly out of his wat'ry cell
To deck great Neptune's diadem.

The Tritons dancing in a ring
Before his palace gates do make
The water with their echoes quake,
Like the great thunder sounding:
The sea-nymphs chant their accents shrill,
And the sirens, taught to kill
    With their sweet voice,
Make ev'ry echoing rock reply
Unto their gentle murmuring noise
The praise of Neptune's empery.

---

[1] The text printed below is taken from the Doubleday edition of Campion's poems (*The Works of Thomas Campion*, ed. Walter R. Davis. Garden City NY: Doubleday, 1967). The text actually used at Oxford differs slightly in spelling and punctuation, and two more substantive variations are identified in the notes below. Some of Campion's own Latin poems can be found in Davis's collection.
[2] The Oxford exercise prints "gliding."
[3] The Oxford exercise prints "sea-god."

Neptune, who *coerces*[4] the swelling waves of the sea
With a nod, your power
Let us sing: how through high mountains
Rivers[5] bring back to you the just *tributes*[6] of the *waters*,[7]

(And) how, *obeying*[8] your laws,
The scaly flocks
Wander safely through the sea's
blue-green fields, (as a) pious band.

And in fact each year every god of the sea
Gleams[9] to have added a gem[10]
To the gems of your splendid crown, great father,[11]
From the glassy seats.

Look! Before the gates of (your) watery home,
Tritons[12] dance in a circle with the sound of their feet;
The deep *waters lament*[13]
The *great*[14] uproar.

This the Nereids sing with shrill voice,
and (they sing that) the *Sirens*[15] of Dicte
Bring *death to wandering sailors*,[16] killing
With their melodious songs,

---

[4] Place in the next line.
[5] Place in the next line.
[6] Place in the next line.
[7] *liquus*
[8] *obtempero* + dative
[9] Place in the fourth line.
[10] Place in the third line.
[11] Only "splendid" should be placed in the third line. All other words belong in line two.
[12] Place at the beginning of line three for a fine enjambment.
[13] Use *latex* for "water," a compound form of *gemino*, and place both words in line four.
[14] Place in line three.
[15] Place in the next line.
[16] Place in the previous line.

Filling the *cliffs*[17] with the sweet murmur of the mountains.
The rocks *re-echo*[18] your glory,
Neptune, who *alone rules*[19] the liquid fields
With just authority.

---

[17] *cautes*
[18] *reclamo*
[19] Place in the next line.

SECTION XII: ASCLEPIADIC METERS

Although the Asclepiadic meters (named for the Hellenistic Greek poet Asclepiades[1]) are traditionally taught after the Sapphics and Alcaics, if at all, they are arguably somewhat easier to produce,[2] and some students may prefer to begin their lyric compositions either here or with the hendecasyllables in the next chapter. Horace uses Asclepiadic meters in thirty-four odes, and they are found in several poems of Catullus. The basic building block of this metrical group is the choriamb ($-\cup\cup-$), which expands to form four different lines.

The "Glyconic" (named for Glycon, a Greek poet of uncertain date) is a line of eight syllables that adds a spondee or trochee before the choriamb and an iamb or a pyrrhic after it.

Horace begins his Glyconics with a spondee in every instance but one: *ignis Iliacas domos* (*Carm.* 1.15.36). As Postgate has perceptively demonstrated, the variation has special significance: "this is the concluding verse of a poem with distinctly Homeric colouring," and in Homer "the name Ἴλιος is very frequently treated as if it began with a consonant" (100). Catullus, on the other hand, prefers a trochaic opening (e.g., *magna progenies Iouis*, 34.6) but sometimes substitutes a spondee (e.g., *o Latonia maximi*, 34.5) or even an iamb (e.g., *Dianae sumus in fide*, 34.1). These same variations occur in his Pherecrateans. The old school rule that "in Glyconics there must be a break in the choriambus"[3] is at best misleading and at worst simply false, as the above examples (Hor. *Carm.* 1.15.36 and Cat. 34.6) demonstrate.[4]

---

[1] Asclepiades must have used the meters that bear his name, but the attribution seems curious to modern readers since the poet's extant work consists almost entirely of epigrams. Lloyd-Jones and Parsons do, however, have a Glyconic fragment of Asclepiades in the *Supplementum Hellenisticum* (Berlin, 1983) 215.

[2] Such is the opinion of Lupton, *Lyric Verse Composition* xxv, and it is not without justification.

[3] B. G. Whitfield, *A Classical Handbook for Sixth Forms*, Oxford: Blackwell (1956) 24.

[4] The phenomenon is admittedly not the norm, but it is not so rare as is commonly supposed. 16 of Horace's 196 Glyconics (or 8%) lack a break in the choriamb. Self-contained choriambs are found at 1.3.33; 1.14.4, 16; 3.7.20, 32; 3.13.16; 3.15.15; 3.24.49, 55, 63; 4.1.7; 4.3.1; and 4.13.20. In addition, the choriamb is unbroken at 1.3.37, 1.14.8, and 3.24.53 because of longer words.

The "Pherecratean" line (named for the fifth-century Greek comic poet Pherecrates, its supposed inventor) is nearly identical to the Glyconic but adds only a single, usually long, syllable to the end of the choriamb:

$$- \; \bar{\smile} \; | \; - \; \smile \; \smile \; - \; | \; \bar{\smile}$$

Elision does not occur in any of Horace's thirty-five Pherecrateans, but Catullus allows elision at 61.35 (*arborem implicat errans*), prodelision at 61.85 (*flet quod ire necesse est*), and hiatus in the refrain *o Hymen Hymenaee* (61.5, etc.). In one instance he even turns the choriamb into a molossus (*nutriunt umore*, 61.25), but this irregularity is best not repeated.

The so-called "lesser Asclepiad" is similar to the Glyconic but has two central choriambs instead of one:

$$- \; \bar{\smile} \; | \; - \; \smile \; \smile \; - \; \| \; - \; \smile \; \smile \; - \; | \; \smile \; \bar{\smile}$$

Maecenas atauis edite regibus

This twelve-syllable line is usually divided exactly in half by a largely inflexible caesura. While the Greek poets generally use a short second syllable, Horace invariably has a long. As such, the first hemistich is equivalent to the first hemistich of a hexameter with a spondaic first foot, e.g., *sic fatur lacrimans*. Similarly, the second hemistich is equivalent to the second half of an Alcaic, e.g., *Postume, Postume*.

The "greater Asclepiad" is another expanded line that inserts an independent choriamb between the two halves of its "lesser" cousin:

$$- \; - \; | \; - \; \smile \; \smile \; - \; \| \; - \; \smile \; \smile \; - \; \| \; - \; \smile \; \smile \; - \; | \; \smile \; \bar{\smile}$$

In this meter both Horace and Catullus always begin with a spondee, but Catullus is more flexible with his caesurae (for which see below).

These four lines, either independently or in various combinations, form the five different classes of Asclepiadic verse used by Horace plus several Catullan meters. Since the numbering system for Asclepiads varies from text to text, little profit is derived from memorizing the names of these meters,[5] but the line combinations

---

[5] For the sake of simplicity, I have followed Nisbet and Hubbard both in the numbering system used (Klingner's) and in the claim that "the names are not worth memorizing" (xxxviii n. 4). It would probably make more sense to number the meters according to the order in which they appear in Horace's *Odes* – a result achieved by transposing the "second" and "fourth" Asclepiads – but no other authority has adopted this system, and I see no reason to compound the confusion by adopting it here.

must be strictly observed, and modern students who wish to emulate the ancients should not allow themselves the license to create their own Asclepiadic variations.

The "First Asclepiad" is a stichic, or "line-" based, meter consisting only of lesser Asclepiads:

$$- \bar{\cup} - \cup \cup - \| - \cup \cup - \cup \bar{\cup}$$

The "Second Asclepiad" is a strophic meter of three lesser Asclepiads and one Glyconic:

$$- \bar{\cup} - \cup \cup - \| - \cup \cup - \cup \bar{\cup}$$
$$- \bar{\cup} - \cup \cup - \| - \cup \cup - \cup \bar{\cup}$$
$$- \bar{\cup} - \cup \cup - \| - \cup \cup - \cup \bar{\cup}$$
$$- \bar{\cup} - \cup \cup - \cup \bar{\cup}$$

The "Third Asclepiad" is also a strophic meter. Lines one and two are lesser Asclepiads, line three is a Pharecratean, and line four is a Glyconic:

$$- \bar{\cup} - \cup \cup - \| - \cup \cup - \cup \bar{\cup}$$
$$- \bar{\cup} - \cup \cup - \| - \cup \cup - \cup \bar{\cup}$$
$$- \bar{\cup} - \cup \cup - \bar{\cup}$$
$$- \bar{\cup} - \cup \cup - \cup \bar{\cup}$$

The "Fourth Asclepiad" strophe combines two identical distichs, each consisting of a Glyconic and a lesser Asclepiad:

$$- \bar{\cup} - \cup \cup - \cup \bar{\cup}$$
$$- \bar{\cup} - \cup \cup - \| - \cup \cup - \cup \bar{\cup}$$
$$- \bar{\cup} - \cup \cup - \cup \bar{\cup}$$
$$- \bar{\cup} - \cup \cup - \| - \cup \cup - \cup \bar{\cup}$$

The "Fifth Asclepiad" is a stichic meter made up only of greater Asclepiadic lines:

$$- - - \cup \cup - \| - \cup \cup - \| - \cup \cup - \cup \bar{\cup}$$

GENERAL REMARKS

Caesurae: Lengthening at the caesura is very rare in Asclepiads and occurs only at 1.13.6 (*manet / umor*) and 3.16.26 (*arat / impiger*).[6] Failure to observe a caesura after six syllables is similarly rare, occurring only at 4.8.17 (*non incendia Karthaginis impiae*) and 2.12.25 (*cum flagrantia detorquet ad oscula*) where the irregularity is felt less strongly since the break falls after a semi-detachable prefix (see Part I). In the greater Asclepiad, Horace omits the tenth-syllable caesura only once: *arcanique Fides prodiga perlucidior uitro* (1.18.16), another case of a semi-detachable prefix, but Catullus treats it as an optional alternative to the sixth-syllable caesura and only requires one strong break in his lines of this type.[7] Elision at the caesura occurs occasionally and is no more or less remarkable here than in any other meter. While the caesura often coincides with a sense break, it also quite commonly falls after a monosyllabic conjunction or a connecting relative pronoun.[8]

Line endings: Horace prefers to end Asclepiadic lines with a word of two or three syllables, but he sometimes uses a four- or five-syllable word, even in the Glyconic and Pherecratean. Not surprisingly, six-syllable endings are comparatively rare but do occur six times in the lesser Asclepiad, once in the greater Asclepiad, and once in the Glyconic.[9] A monosyllable seldom ends an Asclepiadic line, especially if it is not involved in an elision.[10] An unelided monosyllable occurs twice in the lesser Asclepiad (4.13.1, 6) and once in the Pherecratean (1.14.3). The monosyllabic ending is particularly effective at the start of poem 4.13 where the anaphora of *di*, elegantly arranged in a chiasmus, conveys emphasis and excitement:

---

[6] The lengthening of *sibi* at 3.16.21 is of another type because the long second syllable, which reflects an older quantity, is a standard variant.

[7] In poem 30, there are five lines with two regular caesurae (1–3, 5–6), two with a break at six alone (11–12), two at ten alone (4, 7), two at ten with elision at the caesura at six (8, 10), and one at six with elision at ten (9). In just twelve lines, Catullus achieves great metrical variety, which contrasts with the more solemn regularity of Horace.

[8] Nisbet and Hubbard xxxix note that this practice is more common in Asclepiads than in other lyric meters and see it as evidence that the so-called Asclepiadic "caesura" simply marks the division between two separate metrical cola rather than the cutting of a metrical foot. While this assertion is probably true on metrical grounds, placing a caesura after the first word in a clause is sufficiently common in all meters that it need not be rigorously avoided by the modern composer.

[9] 1.1.12, 1.3.20, 1.3.22, 1.36.20, 3.30.4, 4.3.2; 1.18.4; 3.24.53.

[10] In the lesser Asclepiad there is one instance of elision (1.21.14) and two of prodelision (3.25.18, 4.3.24). In the Glyconic there are two instances of elision (1.3.19, 1.19.13) and one of prodelision (4.3.21).

> Audiuere, Lyce, di mea uota, di
> audiuere, Lyce.

Synizesis: In the hexameter, synizesis of certain vowel combinations in Greek words (*eus, ei, eo, eu*) is quite common if not the norm (see Part I), but it does not necessarily occur in the Horatian Asclepiad. Note, for example, Vlixei (1.6.7), Achillei (1.15.34), and Orpheo (1.24.13), where *ei* and *eo* are disyllabic, but Nereus (1.15.5) and Bassareu (1.18.11), where *eu* is treated as a single syllable, as it must be in Greek.

Synaphea: In a lyric stanza, lines tend to share a closer metrical connection than lines in a stichic meter, and the term "synaphea" is used when the principles of elision, hiatus, and lengthening by position are applied across line divisions to create, in effect, a single continuous line. While Horace's Asclepiad stanzas are not written in strict synaphea any more than his Sapphics or Alcaics, the poet rarely ends an Asclepiadic line with a short open vowel (except in poem 1.3 where he does so a remarkable eleven times!) and even less frequently has hiatus between lines.[11] Further, he prefers to end the Glyconic and Pherecratean either with a naturally long syllable or with one that could be lengthened by the first word in the next line (as if the two lines were in synaphea).[12] Catullus always ends his Glyconics in this way.

Arrangement of Words: Ending the two halves of a lesser Asclepiad with a noun and adjective or adjective and noun in agreement is an elegant way to balance the line and is akin to the elegists' similar practice in the pentameter (see page 94), e.g., *et pro sollicitis // non tacitus reis* (4.1.14).

Finer Points On Each Meter

The First Asclepiad: While sentences typically span several lines, Horace often makes his major sense breaks correspond with line endings or, less frequently, with the caesura. If we accept the punctuation of the Oxford Classical Text, full stops are more likely to occur at the end of even-numbered lines than odd, but it would be misleading to think of the first Asclepiad as a "distich" in the same sense as the elegiac couplet or even the fourth Asclepiad. Similarly, Horace almost always writes in multiples of four lines (interpolation is suspected in the

---

[11] Postgate 117–118 offers the following statistics about hiatus in the second asclepiad: 6/189 possible instances within the stanza and 4/54 between stanzas. See his *CR* 32 (1918) 25 for more.

[12] See Postgate *CQ* 16 (1922) 29ff. for more.

thirty-four-line 4.8, the only apparent exception), but sense breaks do not necessarily fall at four-line intervals.[13] The enjambment of a single word sometimes occurs and, as in other meters, can be an effective variation. Horace shows some preference for ending the first hemistich with a word of three syllables, often, but not necessarily, preceded by another trisyllable, e.g., *donarem pateras*. Disyllabic endings are the next most common for the hemistich, and quadrisyllables are acceptable as well, e.g., *gaudes carminibus*. Monosyllabic endings are rare: only four instances, all of them in book 4. Horace's practice in the second hemistich shows no discernible difference from the second half of an Alcaic.

The Second Asclepiad: Horace's use of the lesser Asclepiad in this and the other meters corresponds with his general practice described above. The Glyconic, like the Asclepiad, should typically end with a two- or three-syllable word. Horace uses a quadrisyllable seven times (11%) and a five-syllable word only once. Sense breaks often fall at the end of a strophe, but sentences will sometimes extend past a strophe break. Horace occasionally uses the familiar technique of enjambing a single word to express sudden or emphatic action[14] (e.g., the postponement of *conamur* at 1.6.5–9), and it is not uncommon to have a strong sense break at the caesura. Conversely, the caesura may fall where no grammatical pause is felt (e.g., 1.15.19, *tamen, heu // serus!* and elsewhere in the poem). Sense pauses elsewhere in the strophe are comparatively rare but nonetheless legitimate. (Compare Horace's practice in Sapphic and Alcaic stanzas.)

The Third Asclepiad: The Third Asclepiad is structured somewhat like an Alcaic and can be effectively used for poems of dignified tone (e.g., "O Fons Bandusiae," 3.13), but it is also suited to lighter subjects like the Chloë ode (1.23). While the stanza is sometimes a single sentence, the Pyrrha ode (1.5) shows Horace's skill in extending sentences beyond the stanza breaks when he wants to. In this poem, the only stanza that ends a sentence is the last, and the extreme variation may suggest Pyrrha's lack of constancy.[15] In the grand hymn to Diana (1.21), however, Horace prefers a more stately regularity. The sequence of Pherecratean and Glyconic in the Third Asclepiad can have a pleasant cadence and is well suited to, if not reflective of, the gentle sound of trickling water at 3.13.15–16,

---

[13] Nisbet and Hubbard hypothesize that 1.1 consists of "eight four-line stanzas framed by two distichs" (xlvii), but two- and four-line units seem to play no part in the architecture of 3.30.

[14] See part I.

[15] Compare Horace's similar practice in 1.14 (the "ship of state") where the variation of sentence and stanza breaks may suggest the vicissitudes of seafaring and of politics.

where the repetition of *c, i*, and *l* sounds reinforces the effect: *unde loquaces / lymphae desiliunt tuae.*[16]

The Fourth Asclepiad: The Fourth Asclepiad, Horace's favorite, is traditionally classified as a strophic meter because major sense breaks tend to fall at the end of four-line units. Nevertheless, the distich of Glyconic and lesser Asclepiad has a certain unity, and the only instance of synaloepha in the Asclepiad system occurs between these two lines:

> cur facunda parum decor(o)
> > inter uerba cadit lingua silentio? (4.1.35–6).

In this instance, the hypermeter may imitate the poet's faltering speech as he thinks of Ligurinus.

The Fifth Asclepiad: The Fifth Asclepiad tends to be used for shorter poems. Of Horace's three examples, two consist of eight lines, one of sixteen, and Catullus's only greater Asclepiad has twelve lines. (Note that even though this is a stichic meter, both poets prefer to write in multiples of four, just as Horace did in the First Asclepiad.) Sense breaks are most likely to fall either at the end of a line, especially every fourth line, or at the first caesura, but other pauses are also possible. The central choriamb is often a small syntactic unit unto itself such as a vocative (*Leuconoe, Bacche pater*), a short clause (*uina liques, dum loquimur*), or a parenthetical remark (*scire nefas*). Nisbet and Hubbard claim that "to write in choriambs is something of a *tour de force*" (1.136), so the modern composer may take some satisfaction in success at the greater Asclepiad.

Priapean Verse: Priapean verse, so named because hymns to Priapus were composed in this meter, consists of a Glyconic and a Pherecratean and is used by Catullus in poem 17.

$$- \bar{\smile} - \smile \smile - \smile \bar{\smile} \parallel - \bar{\smile} - \smile \smile - \bar{\smile}$$

The Priapean "distich" is written in strict synaphea (elision occurs four times, hiatus never), so the two lines are often written as one; however, synaphea is not observed between these combined lines.

---

[16] See the comments of L. P. Wilkinson at *GLA* 56–7 and *HLP* 141. Compare also Horace, *Epodes* 16.48: *leuis crepante lympha desilit pede.*

Catullan Stanzas: Catullus 34, a hymn to Diana, employs stanzas of three Glyconics and a Pherecratean. In the epithalamium, poem 61, he expands the stanza to four Glyconics and a Pherecratean. Within his strophes, Catullus observes the principle of synaphea more rigorously than Horace, allowing elision six times (34.11, 23; 61.115, 135, 140, 184), avoiding hiatus,[17] and never ending with a short open vowel. In two instances he even divides a word between two lines: *ama-/tis* (61.46–7) and *Au-/runcleia* (61.82–3).[18] Synaphea does not extend between strophes, and hiatus and short vowels do occur in these positions.

HORATIAN POEMS IN THESE METERS:

1. The First Asclepiad: *C.* 1.1; 3.30; 4.8.
2. The Second Asclepiad: *C.* 1.6, 15, 24, 33; 2.12; 3.10, 16; 4.5, 12.
3. The Third Asclepiad: *C.* 1.5, 14, 21, 23; 3.7, 13; 4.13.
4. The Fourth Asclepiad: *C.* 1.3, 13, 19, 36; 3.9, 15, 19, 24, 25, 28; 4.1, 3.
5. The Fifth Asclepiad: *C.* 1.11, 18; 4.10.

CATULLAN POEMS: 17 (Priapean), 30 (greater Asclepiad), 34 (stanzas of three Glyconics and a Pherecratean), and 61 (stanzas of four Glyconics and a Pherecratean).

---

[17] In the refrain, *io* is monosyllabic (see Fordyce *ad* 117) with the *i* having consonantal force to prohibit hiatus between the Glyconic and Pherecratean. Hiatus after the exclamation is standard.

[18] The text of *amatis* is suspect, for which see Fordyce *ad loc.*, but it probably became "suspect" in the first place because of a misunderstanding of the meter.

EXERCISE XLIII: ASCLEPIADIC SCANSION

Scan two of Horace's most famous odes from book 1. The first (14) is a third Asclepiad and the second (11) is a fifth. Memorization can be an effective way to develop an ear for Horatian rhythm, and it is difficult to find two better specimens than these.

1.14   O nauis, referent in mare te noui
        fluctus. o quid agis? fortiter occupa
           portum. nonne uides ut
               nudum remigio latus,

        et malus celeri saucius Africo
        antemnaeque gemant ac sine funibus
           uix durare carinae
               possint imperiosius

        aequor? non tibi sunt integra lintea,
        non di, quos iterum pressa uoces malo.
           quamuis Pontica pinus,
               siluae filia nobilis,

        iactes et genus et nomen inutile:
        nil pictis timidus nauita puppibus
           fidit. tu, nisi uentis
               debes ludibrium, caue.

        nuper sollicitum quae mihi taedium,
        nunc desiderium curaque non leuis,
           interfusa nitentis
               uites aequora Cycladas.

1.11   Tu ne quaesieris (scire nefas) quem mihi, quem tibi
finem di dederint, Leuconoe, nec Babylonios
temptaris numeros. ut melius, quicquid erit, pati!
seu pluris hiemes seu tribuit Iuppiter ultimam,
quae nunc oppositis debilitat pumicibus mare
Tyrrhenum, sapias, uina liques et spatio breui
spem longam reseces. dum loquimur, fugerit inuida
aetas: carpe diem, quam minimum credula postero.

EXERCISE XLIV: JUMBLED ASCLEPIADS

Unscramble the following phrases and clauses to form proper Asclepiadic units.
Lines 1–15 are lesser Asclepiads, 16–25 are Glyconics, 26–30 are Pherecrateans,
and 31–35 are greater Asclepiads.

1. ambitiosior hederis lasciuis
2. Pelea paene datum Tartaro narrat
3. beatior rege Persarum uigui
4. uiuere tecum amem, libens tecum obeam
5. uicarius sorte aequali recreat
6. hospites et consortem socium fallat
7. uertere fraxinos proceras manibus
8. nox quoque merita nenia dicetur
9. proelia Caesaris historiis dices
10. et spargere nebulam stellis candidis
11. cur fistula cum lyra tacita pendet
12. non marmora incisa notis publicis
13. tendere Lesboum barbiton refugit
14. fraude mala ignem gentibus intulit
15. dente labris memorem notam impressit
16. nil ardui est mortalibus
17. Tydiden parem superis
18. filia siluae nobilis
19. puluere crines collines
20. grata proteruitas urit
21. saeua mater Cupidinum
22. lyrae Romanae fidicen
23. cinge tempora floribus
24. pandite claustra ianuae

153

25. annuit omnibus omnia

26. Luna dicta lumine

27. in amorem inducens

28. beatum Thyna merce

29. et docentes peccare

30. dicens uri ignibus

31. O potens muneribus Veneris et adhuc crudelis

32. quotiens te alterum speculo uideris, "heu" dices

33. sollicitudines mordaces aliter diffugiunt

34. Bacche pater, quis non potius te, teque Venus decens?

35. et Gloria tollens plus nimio uerticem uacuum

EXERCISE XLV: ASCLEPIADIC STANZAS

Translate the following English phrases and clauses into Latin that scans in an Asclepiadic meter. Vocabulary is provided but not in the required word order. Exercises 1–5 are single lesser Asclepiads, and number 6 combines two such lines without specifying line division. Exercise 7 consists of three greater Asclepiads, and excercises 8–10 are second, third, and fourth Asclepiadic strophes respectively. Grammatical hints are given in brackets, and words in parentheses are not to be translated.

1. The human race rushes through forbidden wickedness.
   per nefas uetitum gens humana ruo

2. The hunter forgetful of his tender wife . . .
   uenator immemor tenera coniunx

3. And the muse powerful over the peaceful lyre forbids . . .
   -que Musa potens imbellis lyra ueto

4. Banish the pride hateful to Venus.
   pono superbia ingrata Venus

5. Nevertheless, annoying poverty is absent.
   tamen importuna pauperies absum

6. And yet I do not intend to break you like a savage tigress or Gaetulian lion.
   atqui non ego persequor frango tu ut aspera tigris Gaetulusue leo

7. As often as you look at your changed self in the mirror, you will say, "Alas! Why did I not have as a boy [use *sum* + the dative of possession] the same mind which I have today, or why do my cheeks not return unchanged to these spirits (I now have)."

   quotiens uideo tu alter speculum dico heu
   cur non sum puer eadem mens que est hodie
   uel cur non redeo genae incolumes hi animi

155

8. Anxiety and a hunger for greater things [obj. gen.] follows money (as it grows). By right did I shudder to raise my head to be seen far and wide, Maecenas, glory of the equestrians.

   cura maioraque fames sequor pecunia crescens. ius perhorreo tollo vertex conspicuus late, Maecenas decus eques.

9. Neither Coan purple (garments) nor precious jewels now bring back to you the times which the winged day has once enclosed, buried in the almanac known (to all).

   nec Coae purpureae nec cari lapides iam refero tu tempora quae semel uolucris dies includo condita noti fasti.

10. In a more timely way, you will join in a Bacchic procession to the home of Paulus Maximus, swift on your royal swans, if you seek to burn a suitable heart.

    tempestiue comissor in domus Paulus Maximus ales purpurei olores si quaero torreo idoneum iecur.

EXERCISE XLVIA: ASCLEPIADS
FROM A PARAPHRASE

Translate the following verses of George Hughes (a minor but not untalented Victorian poet) into lines of the First Asclepiad. A paraphrase of a rendering by Benjamin Hall Kennedy (author of the famous *Kennedy's Latin Grammar* and a distinguished versifier in his day) is provided.

> Painter, if thou canst safely gaze
> on all the wonders of that face,
> if thou hast skill to guard the heart
> secure by secrets of thy art,
> o teach that mighty charm, that we
> may gaze securely too, like thee.

> If you can gaze[1] placidly[2], with fixed sight,[3] at
> This face, painter, and nevertheless not be burned,[4]
> Say, o say to (this) student by what arts
> I might *gaze*, like you, and nevertheless not *burn*.[5]

---

[1] *conspicio*
[2] Use an adjective in agreement with the subject.
[3] *lumen* – "light," "eye"
[4] *uro*
[5] *conspicio, ardeo* – remember to use subjunctives.

Exercise XLVIb

Translate the following poem by Thomas Moore into Latin stanzas of the Second Asclepiad. A paraphrase of J. P. Postgate's rendering is provided.

> Come, take thy harp; 'tis vain to muse
> Upon the gathering ills we see;
> Oh! take the harp and let me lose
> All thoughts of ill in hearing thee.
> Sing to me, love! – Though death were near,
> Thy song would make my soul forget –
> Nay, nay, in pity dry that tear,
> All may be well, be happy yet.
> Let me but see that snowy arm
> Once more upon the dear harp lie,
> And I will cease to dream of harm,
> Will smile at fate, while thou art nigh.
> Give me that strain of mournful touch
> We used to love long, long ago,
> Before our hearts had known as much
> As now alas! they bleed to know.

Hurry to take up the hanging *harp*.[1]
In vain you think about how many sad things come together.
O strike the lyre and hold us by your
Voice[2] deaf *to*[3] bad things.

Begin your songs, my life, *if you are going to sing*,[4] and
(Do it for me,) forgetful of nearby *death*.[5] Who knows whether –

---

[1] Three different words for "lyre" will be needed in this poem: *barbitos*, *fides*, and *plectrum*.

[2] Use a poetic plural.

[3] *ad*

[4] Lit. "if you are singing," cf. Martial's *fac si facis* (1.461).

[5] Place in the previous line.

Spare your tears I pray, I pray – the god *will return*[6] *all things*[7]
Back into[8] *a happy state.*[9]

Grant that[10] *I see*[11] again added to your snowy arms
The beloved lyre-string, nor *will I*, wretched, *wish*[12] further
For harsh things. No *need*[13] will be feared
When you are present.[14]

Return those lovable rhythms which for me *and*[15] for you
The lyre moves more tearfully,
Which (thing), once known, torments the *hearts*[16]
Of[17] *those well ignorant*[18] *of what is to come.*[19]

[6] Place in the next line.
[7] Place in the previous line.
[8] *uersus in* (not necessarily together or in the same line)
[9] *in laetum* (previous line)
[10] *da* + pres. subj.
[11] Place in the next line.
[12] Place in the next line.
[13] *necessitas* (next line)
[14] Use an ablative absolute.
[15] Use *quos . . . quos*, without a conjunction.
[16] *pectora*
[17] Despite the English rendering, use the dative, as is common in Latin poetry.
[18] *bene nescius* + genitive
[19] *uenturum*

EXERCISE XLVIc

Translate the following poem by Wordsworth into Latin stanzas of the Third Asclepiad. A paraphrase of Thomas Moss's rendering is provided.

> Not seldom, clad in radiant vest,
>   Deceitfully goes forth the Morn;
> Not seldom Evening in the west
>   Sinks smilingly forsworn.
> The smoothest seas will sometimes prove
>   To the confiding bark untrue;
> And if she trust the stars above,
>   They can be treacherous too.
> The umbrageous oak in pomp outspread,
>   Full oft, when storms the welkin rend,
> Draws lightening down upon the head
>   It promised to defend.

> Often *clad*[1] in rosy colors
> Deceitful Phosphorus goes forth; setting
>   Beneath the shadows, even you often
>   Smile at the treacherous one, Hesperus.
> There is the pine *ship*[2] which, *trusting in*[3] the *false*[4] fidelity of the sea,
> Condemns the *Atlantic*[5] waters for *deceit*[6]
>   And which is deceived by the stars
>   Of the sky, not *trusting well.*[7]

[1] *indutus*
[2] Place in the next line.
[3] *freta* (long *e*), perhaps a pun on *freta* (short *e*) in this context
[4] *composita*, which can also mean "calm," i.e. the false calm, another clever pun on Moss's part
[5] The *a* remains short before *tl*; see Part I.
[6] Use the "genitive of the charge."
[7] In agreement with *pinus*

While the *oak*[8] *promises*[9] hospitality with its spreading *leaves*,[10]
Often when the sky is bristling with *clouds*[11]
<u>Alas it *calls down*</u>[12] <u>dire flames upon the head *trusting in*</u>[13] <u>it</u>.[14]

---

[8] Place in the next line.

[9] *spondeo*

[10] *comae*

[11] Use *polus* for sky and make the whole clause an ablative absolute.

[12] *euoco*

[13] *fisum* + dative

[14] The underlined words represent the last two lines. Entangled word order has made it impossible to specify line divisions.

EXERCISE XLVID

Translate the following lines from Shakespeare (*King Henry VIII*, Act 3, scene1, 3–14) into stanzas of the Fourth Asclepiad. A paraphrase adapted from from the Rev. George Preston's *Exercises in Latin Verse* is provided. Gerard Manley Hopkins translated the same passage into hendecasyllables, and an exercise based on that poem appears in the next chapter.

> Orpheus with his lute made trees,
> And the mountain tops that freeze,
> > Bow themselves, when he did sing:
> To his music plants and flowers
> Ever sprung; as sun and showers
> > There had made a lasting spring.

> Everything that heard him play,
> Even the billows of the sea,
> > Hung their heads, and then lay by,
> In sweet music is such art:
> Killing care and grief of heart
> > Fall asleep or hearing die.

> While *Orpheus*[1] sings, trees
> And *peaks*[2] of mountains *bound*[3] with ice
> > Are bent by the sound of his lyre.
> To Orphic rhythms, flowers spread

> Their buds always, just as in new
> Spring the sun and showers *restore*[4] the day.
> > *You would see*[5] that whatever has heard Orpheus,
> Even the swelling waves,

[1] Following Greek practice, *Orpheus* (nom.) scans as a spondee, but *Orphea* (accusative, line 8) is a dactyl; the scansion cannot be otherwise.
[2] *culmina*
[3] Agrees with "peaks"
[4] *redintegro*
[5] Use the imperfect subjunctive and place in the next line.

162

Reclines with a *weary*[6] *head.*[7]
So much the pleasant music *can do,*[8] which *puts* heavy
    Sorrow *to sleep*[9] and anxious
Cares, or compels them to *die*[10] at the sound.

---

[6] *languescens*
[7] *uertex* (previous line)
[8] *ualeo*
[9] *sopio* (keep in the third line of the stanza)
[10] *inemorior*

EXERCISE XLVIE

Try an exercise as old as the Roman poets themselves: translate the following poem of Anacreon into Latin verse. A paraphrase that will yield distichs of the fourth Asclepiad[1] is provided. As a further exercise, try an unassisted translation into Anacreon's meter: three Glyconics and a Pherecratean.

> Σφαίρῃ δηὖτέ με πορφυρῇ
> βάλλων χρυσοκόμης ῎Ερως
> νήνι ποικιλοσαμβάλῳ
>   συμπαίζειν προκαλεῖται
> ἡ δ᾽, ἐστὶν γὰρ ἀπ᾽ εὐκτίτου
> Λέσβου, τὴν μὲν ἐμὴν κόμην,
> λευκὴ γάρ, καταμέμφεται,
>   πρὸς δ᾽ ἄλλην τινὰ χάσκει.

Cupid, blond with respect to his hair of gold, hurling his purple ball against me, has ordered his *companion*[2] to *contrive*[3] games with a tender maiden adorned with multi-colored sandals. But the maiden, a noble daughter from paternal cities and from her own Lesbos, looks down upon me because shameful white is in my hair, (and), gaping at *some other man*[4] instead of me, *she is carried off.*[5]

---

[1] Note that this poem is not written in the four-line stanzas that Horace favors.

[2] *compar*, with the force of "the man who is 'just right' for the girl whom he is not going to get"

[3] *nectere*

[4] *uir nescioquis* — in Anacreon's poem, the girl is in love with another girl, but the Victorian translator has changed ἄλλην to ἄλλον to make her lover a man (an alteration that D. A. Campbell calls "irresponsible").

[5] *fero*

164

EXERCISE XLVIF

Translate the following poem by Sir William Watson into the meter of Catullus 34 (three Glyconics and a Pherecratean), following the Latin rendering of E. D. Stone. The poem is not a particularly distinguished specimen of English literature, but Stone's rendering is rather good and provides a rare chance to practice a Catullan meter seldom used by modern poets. Stanza divisions are given in the paraphrase, but line divisions are impossible to provide.

> April, April,
> Laugh thy girlish laughter;
> Then, the moment after,
> Weep thy girlish tears!
> April, that mine ears
> Like a lover greetest,
> If I tell thee, sweetest,
> All my hopes and fears,
> April, April,
> Laugh thy golden laughter,
> But, the moment after,
> Weep thy golden tears!

First imbue the sky with the girlish laughter of April; then moisten your face with girlish tears.

April, similar to a *suitor*[1], *sound upon*[2] my ears. If, sweetest, I will have said what *I hope or fear*[3]

You are, respond, good divinity, to me with golden laughter, then right away *weep*[4] with golden *teardrops*.[5]

---

[1] *procus* (a good Horatian word used at 3.10.11, an Asclepiad) — gen. needed with *similis*
[2] *adsono* + dative
[3] Remember to use subjunctives.
[4] *illacrimor*
[5] *guttae*

SECTION XIII: THE HENDECASYLLABIC METER

Once the Sapphic, Alcaic, and Asclepiadic meters have been mastered, the hendecasyllablic or "Phalaecian" meter (named for the fourth-century Greek poet Phalaecus, who was the first to use it as a stichic meter[1]) will seem relatively easy. Although Horace wrote no hendecasyllabic poems, it was the favorite meter of Catullus (used in forty poems) and is found in the works of Martial and Statius as well. The rhythmic pattern is quite straightforward: a spondee, a dactyl, and three trochees, the last of which may be exchanged for a spondee:

$$\text{--} \;\text{--} \; | \; \text{--} \; \cup \; \cup \; | \; \text{--} \; \cup \; | \; \text{--} \; \cup \; | \; \text{--} \; \; \smile$$

cui do - no le -pi - dum no - uum li - bel - lum

Catullus sometimes begins with a trochee or iamb but not as frequently as in his Glyconics and Pherecrateans. Martial and Statius always use the spondaic opening, a preference unnecessarily shared by most modern composers and school texts. In Catullus 55 and 58b, a spondee occasionally replaces the dactyl of the second foot, e.g., *oramus si forte non molestum est* (55.1). As Fordyce rightly implies, this experimental variation comes off well in the "lively, playful" 55 but fails in the "clumsy" 58b (226).

Properly speaking, the hendecasyllabic line has no fixed caesura, but a word break in the middle of the third foot is quite common, e.g., *lugete, o Veneres // Cupidinesque* and *Annales Volusi // cacata carta* (Cat. 3.1, 36.1); *Stella delicium // mei columbae* (Mart. 1.7.1); *quis duri silicis // grauisque ferri* (Stat. *Siluae* 4.3.1). This "caesura" sometimes falls after a monosyllabic connecting word, preposition, or exclamatory *o*, e.g., *soles occidere et // redire possunt* (Cat. 5.4), *uelles dicere nec // tacere posses* (6.3), *Varus me meus ad // suos amores* (10.1), *qualecumque; quod, o // patrona uirgo* (1.9). When there is no such caesura in the third foot, the poets generally favor a word break at the end of the second foot, e.g., *uiuamus mea / Lesbia atque amemus* (5.1). Elision at either pause is acceptable although not common, e.g., *puluinusque perae (-que) // et hic et ille* (Cat. 6.9), *uisam te incolum (-em) // audiamque Hiberum* (9.6). Failure to have a pause after

---

[1] The so-called "Phalaecian" hendecasyllable goes back at least to Anacreon (fr. 33 D) and was also used by Sophocles, either in its "standard" form (e.g., *Ajax* 634), with various syllables transposed [for which see Dale, *Lyric Metres of Greek Drama* (Cambridge, 1968) 141], or combined with a Glyconic as a single metrical unit (e.g., *Phil.* 855–856).

166

either five or six syllables is relatively rare but nevertheless legitimate: only 13 out of 517 lines in Catullus (= 2.5%) but somewhat more frequent in the later writers.[2] No vowels are irregularly lengthened at either central pause, but correption and hiatus occur at the end of the second foot: *deferri. manë inquii puellae* (Cat. 10.27) and *malest me herculë et laboriose* (38.2).[3]

As in the hexameter, it was considered inelegant to allow the frequent correspondence of word and foot divisions in the hendecasyllable, and lines like *densas flammeus orbis inter umbras* and *Poenos Bagrada serpit inter agros* (Stat. *Siluae* 1.6.87, 4.3.91), in which each word occupies its own foot, were avoided.[4] Other lines in which no foot is divided by a word break are similarly rare but do occur:

> omnes | unius | aestimemus | assis (Cat. 5.4)
> natum | dicitur | esse | comparasti (10.15)
> tollis | lintea | neglegentiorum (12.3)
> Caeli | Lesbia | nostra | Lesbi (-a) | illa (58.1).

In Catullus, the hendecasyllable very frequently begins with a word of one or two syllables, but a trisyllable is not uncommon. Longer words are comparatively rare but acceptable: quadrisyllables occur about 2% of the time, quinquesyllables 1.5%, and a six-syllable word only once – the nicely exotic three-word line, *lasarpiciferis iacet Cyrenis* (7.4).[5] Lines in which a caesura is found typically end in one of three ways:

$\parallel \cup - \mid \cup - \breve{\cup}$	nouum libellum
$\parallel \cup - \cup \mid - \breve{\cup}$	redire possunt
$\parallel \cup - \cup \breve{\cup}$	Cupidinesque.

Without a caesura, a quadrisyllable is usually involved:

$- \cup \mid - \cup - \breve{\cup}$	esse neglegentem
$- \cup - \cup \mid - \breve{\cup}$	explicare cartis.

---

[2] Crusius 104 gives the statistic of 36/456 (= 7.9%) in Statius.

[3] Note, however, that hiatus with interjections is not especially unusual: cf. Cat. 3.16 and see Part I.

[4] Postgate 99, citing only the first of these lines as if it were the only example, claims that the close syntactic relationship of *inter* and *umbras* softens the effect. Perhaps so, but such lines are nevertheless quite rare and probably should not be emulated.

[5] Elided syllables are discounted in these calculations, i.e. *adest(e) hendecasyllabi* is considered a disyllabic opening.

The frequency of these endings should not discourage the occasional use of others, but six-syllable endings are rare (only eight instances or about 1.5%), and only once does a seven-syllable word end a line — the remarkable two-word *argutatio inambulatioque* (6.11). Monosyllabic endings other than the prodelision of *est* are also rare but seem to carry no special connotations. The coincidence of accent and vowel quantity is inevitable at the end of a hendecasyllable, and Statius seems to have preferred it at the beginning of the line as well, but Catullus felt free to violate the principle by sometimes starting with a self-contained iamb (usually a possessive adjective like *meus*), which by definition conflicts with accent. In all other respects, the hendecasyllable is a relatively regular meter in which certain variations or irregularities such as hypermetric lines and the irrational lengthening of vowels simply do not occur. Synizesis is rare but follows the same principles as in other meters. There is also one instance of a consonantal *i* in Catullus: the trisyllabic *Camerium* (55.10).

Readers of Vergil and Horace will be quite comfortable to find adjectives placed at some from the nouns they modify, and the same phenomenon occurs in Catullus, who seems to have been one of the earliest poets to employ the technique on a regular basis. Some preliminary word order research of Donka Markus suggests a further stylistic feature of Catullan lyric verse: When Catullus uses a "discontinuous noun phrase" of the pattern adjective—verb—noun (with or without intervening words), the noun almost always marks the end of a thought, either as a transition to a related idea, a point of contrast with the idea that follows, or a sign of closure at the end of a sentence or poem.[6] It should be noted, however, that the principle does not work in reverse, for the poet will often employ other verbal patterns at points of transition, contrast, or closure.

6 "A Century of Advances in Latin Word-Order Studies and What They Mean for Latin Pedagogy," *ACL Institute*, 30 June 2001

EXERCISE XLVII: HENDECASYLLABIC SCANSION

Scan Catullus 50, marking foot divisions and noting elisions when they occur. Other subtleties of versification should also be observed.

> Hesterno, Licini, die otiosi
> multum lusimus in meis tabellis,
> ut conuenerat esse delicatos:
> scribens uersiculos uterque nostrum
> ludebat numero modo hoc modo illoc,
> reddens mutua per iocum atque uinum.
> atque illinc abii tuo lepore
> incensus, Licini, facetiisque,
> ut nec me miserum cibus iuuaret
> nec somnus tegeret quiete ocellos,
> sed toto indomitus furore lecto
> uersarer, cupiens uidere lucem,
> ut tecum loquerer, simulque ut essem.
> at defessa labore membra postquam
> semimortua lectulo iacebant,
> hoc, iucunde, tibi poema feci,
> ex quo perspiceres meum dolorem.
> nunc audax caue sis, precesque nostras,
> oramus, caue despuas, ocelle,
> ne poenas Nemesis reposcat a te.
> est uehemens dea: laedere hanc caueto.

EXERCISE XLVIII: JUMBLED HENDECASYLLABLES

Unscramble the following hendecasyllables. Since most of the lines are taken from Statius, initial spondees predominate, and some final *o*'s are short (see Part I). Elision occurs only in number 17.

1. o quantae manus pariter laborant

2. bone conditor camporum meorum

3. Lucrinum nauiget primo uespere

4. magnus ordo saeculorum manet te

5. nunc Oriens triumphos magnos dabit

6. Aurora nouos ortus uix mouebat

7. cadebant Caryotides praegnates

8. remisit reuerentiam libertas

9. amnes docti largius euagentur

10. sacerdos Romani chori colitur

11. sinu blando recepit Calliope

12. senatum purpureum cantu trahes

13. et Orpheus noster tibi proferetur

14. qualem Venus blanda -que Iuno daret

15. Babylon sepulchro angusto premit

16. in medullis ardet mollibus ignis

17. redde codicillos, proba et pudica (begin with an iamb)

18. ut iubet lex Postumiae magistrae

19. facerem me unum beatiorem

20. et doloris sui solaciolum

EXERCISE IL: THE HENDECASYLLABIC LINE

Translate the following phrases and sentences into hendecasyllables. Vocabulary is provided. Number ten covers three lines, and line divisions are not specified.

1. something sadder than the tears of Simonides
   maestum lacrimae Simonideae

2. but Acme, gently bending back her head . . .
   at Acme leuiter reflectens caput

3. we will fly to the famous cities of Asia
   uolo ad clarae urbes Asia

4. you will show where your shady places are
   demonstro ubi tuae tenebrae sum

5. the crude muse of fierce Ennius will yield
   rudis musa ferox Ennius cedo

6. O Fates too cruel and harsh . . .
   o Parca nimium saeua -que grauis

7. with the shining plectrum he brushed away (her) tears
   nitens plectrum abrado lacrimae

8. you look down upon the lands and laugh at the tombs
   despicio terrae et rideo sepulchra

9. for husbands returning to (their) brides
   mariti redeo ad nuptae

10. in the middle of the arena, a shining ball of fire fell among the
    thick shadows, surpassing the flame of the Gnosian crown

    media harena nitens flammeus orbis descendo inter densae um-brae uincens fax Cnosiaca corona

EXERCISE LA: HENDECASYLLABLES
FROM A PARAPHRASE

Translate the following poem by Herrick into Latin hendecasyllables. A paraphrase of J. P. Postgate's rendering is provided.

> Smooth was the sea and seem'd to call
> Two prettie girles to play withall;
> Who padling there, the sea soone frown'd
> And on a sudden both were drown'd.
> What credit can we give to seas,
> Who, kissing, kill such Saints as these?

> The face of the sea was smiling, and two
> Charming girls it calls to games.
> But soon, while they delight to play *in*[1] the waves,
> It shakes its brow and *wrinkles its face,*[2]
> And suddenly it has devoured both in the *seething tide.*[3]
> What faith *will there be*[4] for you, Neptune,
> You who kill such (girls) but *by kissing*[5] (them)?

[1] *per*
[2] Idiomatic: *rugas trahere* ("to lead forth wrinkles")
[3] *aestus*
[4] *futura est*
[5] Use the gerund.

EXERCISE LB

While travelling in Austria, Francis William Pember saw a witty "Inscription on a Beer-Tun at an Inn at Waidbrück in Tirol," which he translated into Latin hendecasyllables. Follow his example from a paraphrase.

> Trinkt so lang das Becher winkt,
> Trinket alle Tage!
> Ob Mann im Jenzeit auch noch trinkt,
> Das is eine Frage![1]

While the *cup*[2] *nods at*[3] us, let us drink,
Furius! However many days go by, let us drink!
Let us drink, since it is in doubt, *isn't it*,[4]
When *we will have crossed over*[5] to many more!

---

[1] "Drink as long as the cup beckons; drink every day! Whether one also drinks in the hereafter, that is a question!"

[2] *scyphus*

[3] *innuo* + dat.

[4] *an non*

[5] *transmeo*

EXERCISE LC

Translate these lines from Shakespeare (previously used in an Asclepiadic exercise) into Latin hendecasyllables. A. E. Housman praised the rendering of Hopkins, which is paraphrased below.

> Orpheus with his lute made trees,
> And the mountain tops that freeze,
> Bow themselves, when he did sing:
> To his music plants and flowers
> Ever sprung; as sun and showers
> There had made a lasting spring.
>
> Everything that heard him play,
> Even the billows of the sea,
> Hung their heads, and then lay by,
> In sweet music is such art:
> Killing care and grief of heart
> Fall asleep or hearing die.

With his singing Orpheus is said *to have summoned*[1] both the trees
And the mountains sluggish with snow.
If he had played anything, the grapes of the vine,
Plants, flowers he immediately brought back.
You would say that the Zephyrs and Apollo for him
Had acted together *for*[2] a more serene day
And that everlasting spring continued.
Then the winds *calmed,*[3] then
Every wave settled back from the *compliant*[4] sea.

---

[1] Place in the next line.
[2] *in diem* (idiomatic)
[3] Use the syncopated perfect of *pono*.
[4] *obsequens*

This is the empire of art and of the Muse:
What[5] more *troublesome*[6] and sicker *care*
Had *recently*[7] existed, *it is necessary*[8]
To silence *with a speaking plectrum*[9] or to die.

[5] Place in the next line with *cura*.
[6] *importunus*
[7] Place in the previous line.
[8] Place in the next line.
[9] Place in the previous line.

EXERCISE LD

As a final exercise, try to turn Tennyson's English "Hendecasyllables" into Latin of the same meter. It has been done by John F. Davies, so a good solution is possible.

O you chorus of indolent reviewers,
Irresponsible indolent reviewers –
Look, I come to the test, a tiny poem,
All composed in a metre of Catullus:
All in quantity, careful of my motion,
Like the skater on ice that hardly bears him,
Lest I fall unawares before the people,
Waking laughter in indolent reviewers.
Should I flounder awhile, without a tumble,
Through this metrification of Catullus,
They should speak to me not without a welcome,
All that chorus of indolent reviewers.
Hard, hard, hard it is, only not to tumble,
So fantastical is the dainty metre.
Wherefor slight me not wholly, nor believe me
Too presumptuous, indolent reviewers.
O blatant magazines, regard me rather –
Since I blush to belaud myself a moment –
As some rare little rose, a piece of inmost
Horticultural art, or half-coquette like
Maiden, not to be greeted unbenignly.

SECTION XIV: IAMBIC METERS

Students of Greek verse composition typically learn iambics first, but Latin iambics are often neglected entirely and comprise a statistically insignificant percentage of all original Latin poems published in the last hundred and fifty years. In ancient Rome, however, iambic meters were much more common and were used for comic and tragic dialogue as well as for several of the lyric compositions of Catullus and Horace. They therefore merit at least some consideration. The basic iambic measure is the trimeter, but there are also dimeters, senarii, pure iambics, choliambics, pythiambics, galliambics, and catalectic forms. Each of these will be discussed in turn, but a detailed analysis of dramatic usage falls outside the scope of this guide, which follows tradition and emphasizes the lyric meters upon which most modern iambic compositions are based.

The Greek poet Archilochus is said to have originated the iambic meter, which takes its name from the verb ἰαμβιάζειν ("to lampoon") and is also related to the verb ἰάπτειν ("to shoot" or "hurl"). The invective character of Archilochan iambics is readily apparent in such verses as ἥδε δ᾽ ὥστ᾽ ὄνου ῥάχις / ἕστηκεν ὕλης ἀγρίης ἐπιστεφής ["but this (island) stands like the backbone of an ass crowned with a wild wood" – a critique of the rugged terrain on the island of Thasos] or ἡ δέ οἱ σάθη / ὡσεί τ᾽ ὄνου Πριηνέος / κήλωνος ἐπλήμμυρεν ὀτρυγηφάγου (better left untranslated). Horace reflects an awareness of the etymology of "iamb" in his line, *Archilochum proprio rabies armauit iambo* (*AP* 79).

1. **Iambic Trimeter**: The iambic trimeter is the root of several iambic meters and is, from the standpoint of Latin verse composition, the most important pattern to learn. The Latin trimeter is most closely related to the iambics of Greek tragedy and consists of three pairs of iambic feet. Numerous substitutions are possible, particularly in the odd-numbered feet, and the full range of variants is schematized as follows:

$$\overset{\smile\smile}{=}\; \underset{\smile}{=}\; |\; \smile\; \underset{\smile}{=}\; |\; \overset{\smile\smile}{=}\; \underset{\smile}{=}\; |\; \smile\; \underset{\smile}{=}\; |\; \overset{\smile\smile}{=}\; -\; |\; \smile\; \underset{\smile}{}$$

A less compressed diagram offers a slightly more precise perspective on the line:

```
 ⏑ ‒  | ⏑ ‒ | ⏑ ‒ | ⏑ ‒  | ⏑ ‒ | ⏑ ‒
 ‒ ‒  |   ⊢ ‒ |     | ‒ ‒ |
```

∪⏑⏑ | ∪⏑⏑| ∪⏑⏑ | ∪⏑⏑ | | ∪ ∪

– ⏑⏑| |– ⏑⏑| | |

⏑⏑– | | ⏑⏑ –| | ⏑⏑–|

⏑⏑⏑⏑| | | |

Note that in each foot except the last two, the long syllable may be resolved into two shorts, but a long first syllable is possible only in feet one, three, and five, which are sometimes called "heavy" for this reason. That initial long syllable may also be resolved into two shorts to produce an anapest.

Although many substitutions are theoretically possible, Horace allows himself a relatively narrow range of departures from the basic iambic rhythm. A spondee is the most likely variant in the odd-numbered feet, and dactyls, anapests, and tribrachs are comparatively rare and are often used to accommodate proper names, e.g., *Canidia breuibus illigata uiperis* (*Ep.* 5.15). Confining the table to the most common variations yields the pattern ⊽ – | ∪ – | ⊽ – | ∪ – | ⊽ – | ∪ ⊽. Lines consisting of iambs and one or two spondees are plentiful, e.g.,

at o deorum quidquid in caelo regit (∪ – | ∪ – | ∪ – | ∪ – | – – | ∪ ⌣),
ut haec trementi questus ore constitit (∪ – | ∪ – | – – | ∪ – | ∪ –| ∪ ⌣), and
horret capillis ut marinus asperis (– – | ∪ – | – – | ∪ – | ∪ – | ∪ ⌣),

but Horace seldom has spondees in all three of the odd feet, e.g., *longo die bis terque mutatae dapis* (– – | ∪ – | – – | ∪ – | – – | ∪ ⌣).

The iambic trimeter is divided by a "strong" caesura in either the third or fourth foot, but the penthimimeral (third foot) variety is much more common, e.g., *inutilisque // falce ramos amputans* (*Ep.* 2.13) but *ut gaudet insitiua // decerpens pira* (*Ep.* 2.19). As in other meters, the caesura may fall after *et* or other conjunctions, e.g., *libenter hoc et // omne militabitur* (*Ep.* 1.23). The term "strong" is a somewhat misleading description of this caesura. While it can sometimes fall after a long syllable, e.g., *ut Argonautas // praeter omnis candidum* (3.9), the nature of the iambic meter causes the caesura to fall more frequently after a short syllable, making it "weak," or less pronounced, in recitation (as in the examples from *Epodes* 1 and 2 above). To be more precise: The caesurae that are not allowed are those that follow the first short syllable of a dactyl or anapest, and a tribrach must be divided after the first syllable. Exceptions to this caesura rule are practically non-existent and seem to be confined to instances involving semi-detachable prefixes, e.g., *ut adsidens in- // plumibus pullis auis* (1.19).

Anthon rightly observes that "the accent is of great importance in this meter" and "should fall either on the second syllable of the third foot, or on the second syllables of both the second and fourth feet" (259), e.g.,

> ut gaud|et in|siti|ua de|cerpens | pira (2.19), or
> utrum|ne **ius**|si per|seque|mur otium (1.7).

The trimeter is used for dialogue in Senecan tragedy and as a stichic meter in *Epode* 17. In combination with other lines, it forms the "Iambic System" and Second Pythiambic meter (3 and 4b below).

2. **Iambic Dimeter**: The iambic dimeter consists of two pairs of iambs and admits fewer substitutions than the trimeter:

    $$\breve{u} \; \overset{\smile}{\smile} \; | \; \cup \; \overset{\smile}{\smile} \; | \; \bar{u} - | \cup \; \bar{u}$$

    Spondees are typical in the odd-numbered feet, and a tribrach is sometimes found in the second foot, but an iamb is more common in this position. The line has no regular caesura. The patterns of *ferens olentem Meuium* (10.2) and *porrecta mergos inuenit* (22) are typical.

3. **The "Iambic System"** (sometimes called an "iambic strophe" or "iambic distich") consists of a trimeter and dimeter. It is used in Horace's first ten *Epodes*, e.g.,

    > Beatus ille qui procul negotiis
    > ut prisca gens mortalium (2.1–2).

    Synaphea does not occur in this or any other iambic distich.

4a. **First Pythiambic Meter**: When the dimeter or trimeter combines with a dactylic hexameter (as in *Epodes* 14–16), the meter is called "Pythiambic," so named for Pythia, the priestess of Apollo, who prophesied in hexameters. The first Pythiambic meter consists of a hexameter followed by an iambic dimeter. It is used in *Epodes* 14 and 15, e.g.,

    > Nox erat et caelo fulgebat Luna sereno
    > inter minora sidera (15.1–2).

4b. **Second Pythiambic Meter**: When the hexameter is followed by a trimeter (as in *Epode* 16), the distich is called a Second Pythiambic. In Horace's poem, the trimeter is "pure" (see section 6 below), meaning that no substitutions for the iamb are allowed, e.g.,

    > Altera iam teritur bellis ciuilibus aetas,
    > suis et ipsa Roma uiribus ruit (1–2).

The basic rules of hexameter composition apply in both Pythiambic meters, but Horace is freer than Vergil in his allowance of metrical anomalies, most of which bear no discernible emphasis, e.g., the word break after the second foot in 14.1 (*mollis inertia cur tantam diffuderit imis*) or the monosyllabic endings of 15.17 and 16. 15 (*atque meo nunc, aut melior pars*).

5. **Choliambics**: The choliambic line takes its name from the Greek adjective χωλός (lame) and is also known as a *scazon*, or "limping" verse. It is used eight times by Catullus (8, 22, 31, 37, 39, 44, 59, 60) and can also be found in the works of Martial and in Persius's Prologue. The first four feet follow the pattern of the regular iambic trimeter, but variations tend to be more limited, and resolution of the long syllables into two shorts is relatively uncommon and limited to feet two and three. The full scheme is as follows:

$$\overline{\cup} - \cup \overset{\smile\smile}{=} \quad \overline{\cup} \overset{\smile\smile}{=} \quad \cup - - \overline{\cup}$$

Spondees are generally found in feet one and three, and iambs in feet two and four. The pattern is reversed in the last two feet, with an iamb in the fifth foot and a spondee or trochee in the sixth. This unexpected change in the otherwise regular cadence gives the line the "limping" effect for which it is named, e.g., *Apollinarem conueni meum, scazon* (Martial 7.26.1).

Some of Catullus's best invectives are in the choliambic meter, which he effectively uses to lament his own wretchedness (*Miser Catulle, desinas ineptire*, 8.1), make fun of the poetic pretensions of Suffenus (22), attribute a sudden illness to the "cold" oration of Sestius (44), skewer the sexual exploits of Rufa of Bologna (59), and satirize the perpetual grin of Egnatius, who has some peculiar habits of oral hygiene (37, 39).

6. **Pure Iambics**: The Pure Iambic Trimeter, as its name implies, consists solely of iambs without substitution, except for the frequent allowance of a pyrrhic at the end of the line. Its caesura is entirely regular. Catullus 4 is written in this meter, e.g., *phaselus ille, quem uidetis, hospites* (1), but pure iambic lines can also occur within the regular iambic trimeter, e.g., *paratus omne Caesaris periculum* (*Epodes* 1.3).

7. **Senarii**: In the senarius, or six-foot line, no distinction is made between the odd and even numbered feet, and spondees, dactyls, and anapests are freely allowed in every foot but the last, which remains iambic:
$\overset{\smile\smile}{\smile\smile}|\overset{\smile\smile}{\smile\smile}|\overset{\smile\smile}{\smile\smile}|\overset{\smile\smile}{\smile\smile}|\overset{\smile\smile}{\smile\smile}|\cup\underline{\cup}$. Some lines remain within the rules of the trimeter, e.g., *sum uero et alter // noster est Leonida* ($--\cup--\|-\cup-\cup-\cup-$, Pl.*As.* 58), but variations occur more frequently in the senarius, and lines that are practically devoid of a true iambic cadence are not uncommon, e.g., *sed nimium lepide dissimulant quasi nil sciant* ($-\cup\cup-\cup\cup--\cup\cup-\cup\cup-\cup-$, Pl.

Cas. 771). The senarius is used by Plautus and Terence and is the common meter of all early Roman drama.

8. **Iambic Trimeter Catalectic**: The Iambic Trimeter Catalectic follows the basic pattern of the trimeter but drops the final syllable. Substitutions are mostly limited to spondees in the odd-numbered feet. The iambic trimeter catalectic is never found alone, but Horace combines it with a greater Archilochian in *Odes* 1.4 and a trochaic dimeter catalectic in 2.18 (see the Table of Meters for the patterns).

9. **Galliambics**: The Galliambic meter takes its name from the priests of Cybele called *Galli* (Γάλλοι) and is probably not even "iambic" in origin. Although a mere two Greek Galliambic lines have survived, the meter seems to have been based upon minor ionics (⏑ ⏑ – –), combining a dimeter with a catalectic dimeter.

$$\cup\cup--|\cup\cup-- \quad | \quad \cup\!\!\cup--|\cup\cup-$$

Resolution and contraction (i.e. the substitution of two shorts for a long and vice versa) are possible, and anaclasis (i.e. the rearrangement of longs and shorts within or between feet) can also occur. The metrician Hephaestion makes specific mention of an anaclasis in which the final long syllable of the first ionic is exchanged with the initial short syllable of the second ionic: ⏑ ⏑ – ⏑ | – ⏑ – –. This pattern, which does have something of an iambic cadence to it, is the normal first hemistich of Catullan galliambics. Allowing for resolution and contraction, the full metrical scheme for Catullus is as follows:

$$\overline{\cup\cup}\ \overline{\cup\cup}\cup\ \overline{\cup\cup}\ \cup--\ \|\ \overline{\cup\cup}\ \overline{\cup\cup}\ \cup\ \overline{\cup\cup}\ \overline{\cup\cup}$$

A caesura in the fourth foot is typical, and the majority of Catullan lines follow the model of 63.1: *super alta uectus Attis // celeri rate maria* (⏑ ⏑ – ⏑ – ⏑ – – ‖ ⏑ ⏑ – ⏑ ⏑ ⏑ ⏑ ⏑). Line 5 begins with a long syllable (*deuolsit ili acuto sibi pondera silice*), and two shorts are contracted into a long near the end of line 14 (*aliena quae petentes uelut exules loca*), but resolution is more likely than contraction, e.g., *ubi capita Maenades ui iaciunt hederigerae* (23, first foot) and *simul haec comitibus Attis cecinit notha mulier* (27, second foot). The greatest number of resolved feet occurs in line 63, where the rapid rhythm nicely reflects the anguish and confusion of Attis as he reflects upon his four stages of life – *puer, ephebus, adulescens*, and *mulier*, but never *uir*:

ego mulier, ego adulescens, ego ephebus, ego puer

$$\cup\cup\cup\cup\cup|\cup\cup\cup--\|\cup\cup-\cup\cup\cup\cup$$

Given Latin's 2:1 ratio of long to short syllables, the predominance of shorts required by the galliambic meter is something of a metrical *tour de force*.

A NOTE ON LINE ENDINGS

Monosyllabic endings, including those involving the prodelision of *est*, are extremely rare in Horatian iambics of all types. When an unelided monosyllable does end a line, it is invariably preceded by another. Such endings are limited to five instances in Horace: *Ep.* 4.2 (*discordia est*), 15.12 (*uiri est*), 17.25 (*neque est*), 11.21 (*et heu*), and 17.63 (*in hoc*). Catullus allows the prodelision of *est* with relative freedom in his choliambics, but unelided monosyllabic endings occur only twice, and, as in Horace, they are preceded by other monosyllables: 39.20 (*dens est*), and 44.2 (*non est*). In iambics, two-, three-, and four-syllable endings are the norm, and five-syllable endings, though slightly less common, are entirely regular. A six-syllable ending occurs only once in Horace (4.11, *triumuiralibus*) and never in Catullus, whose scazons are more likely to end with di- or trisyllables.

EXERCISE LI: IAMBIC SCANSION

Scan the following iambic lines and distichs. The required meter is specified for each exercise.

Iambic trimeters from Horace's *Epode* 17

> quid obseratis auribus fundis preces?
> non saxa nudis surdiora nauitis
> Neptunus alto tundit hibernus salo.
> inultus ut tu riseris Cotytia
> uolgata, sacrum liberi Cupidinis,
> et Esquilini pontifex uenefici
> inpune ut Vrbem nomine impleris meo?
> quid proderat ditasse Paelignas anus
> uelociusue miscuisse toxicum?
> sed tardiora fata te uotis manent:
> ingrata misero uita ducenda est in hoc,
> nouis ut usque suppetas laboribus.

Iambic trimeters from Seneca's *Phaedra*

> Compesce amoris impii flammas, precor,
> nefasque quod non ulla tellus barbara
> commisit umquam, non uagi campis Getae
> nec inhospitalis Taurus aut sparsus Scythes;
> expelle facinus mente castifica horridum
> memorque matris metue concubitus nouos.
> miscere thalamos patris et gnati apparas
> uteroque prolem capere confusam impio?
> perge et nefandis uerte naturam ignibus.
> cur monstra cessant? aula cur fratris uacat?

Iambic distichs from Horace's *Epode* 2

> Beatus ille qui procul negotiis,
> ut prisca gens mortalium,

paterna rura bubus exercet suis
solutus omni faenore
neque excitatur classico miles truci
neque horret iratum mare
forumque uitat et superba ciuium
potentiorum limina.
ergo aut adulta uitium propagine
altas maritat populos
aut in reducta ualle mugientium
prospectat errantis greges
inutilisque falce ramos amputans
feliciores inserit
aut pressa puris mella condit amphoris
aut tondet infirmas ouis.

Choliambics from Catullus 8

Miser Catulle, desinas ineptire,
et quod uides perisse perditum ducas.
fulsere quondam candidi tibi soles,
cum uentitabas quo puella ducebat
amata nobis quantum amabitur nulla.
ibi illa multa cum iocosa fiebant,
quae tu uolebas nec puella nolebat,
fulsere uere candidi tibi soles.
nunc iam illa non uult: tu quoque impotens noli,
nec quae fugit sectare, nec miser uiue,
sed obstinata mente perfer, obdura.
uale puella, iam Catullus obdurat,
nec te requiret nec rogabit inuitam.
at tu dolebis, cum rogaberis nulla.
scelesta, uae te, quae tibi manet uita?
quis nunc te adibit? cui uideberis bella?
quem nunc amabis? cuius esse diceris?
quem basiabis? cui labella mordebis?
at tu, Catulle, destinatus obdura.

First Pythiambic distichs from Horace's *Epode* 14

Mollis inertia cur tantam diffuderit imis

obliuionem sensibus,
pocula Lethaeos ut si ducentia somnos
arente fauce traxerim,
candide Maecenas, occidis saepe rogando:
deus, deus nam me uetat
inceptos, olim promissum carmen, iambos
ad umbilicum adducere.

Second Pythiambic distichs from Horace's *Epode* 16

non huc Argoo contendit remige pinus
neque inpudica Colchis intulit pedem,
non huc Sidonii torserunt cornua nautae,
laboriosa nec cohors Vlixei.
nulla nocent pecori contagia, nullius astri
gregem aestuosa torret impotentia.
Iuppiter illa piae secreuit litora genti,
ut inquinauit aere tempus aureum,
aere, dehinc ferro durauit saecula, quorum
piis secunda uate me datur fuga.

Galliambics from Catullus 63

patria o mei creatrix, patria o mea genetrix,
ego quam miser relinquens, dominos ut erifugae
famuli solent, ad Idae tetuli nemora pedem,
ut aput niuem et ferarum gelida stabula forem,
et earum omnia adirem furibunda latibula,
ubinam aut quibus locis te positam, patria, reor?
cupit ipsa pupula ad te sibi derigere aciem,
rabie fera carens dum breue tempus animus est.
egone a mea remota haec ferar in nemora domo?
patria, bonis, amicis, genitoribus abero?
abero foro, palaestra, stadio et gyminasiis?
miser a miser, querendum est etiam atque etiam, anime.

EXERCISE LII: IAMBIC METER IDENTIFICATION

Scansion is more difficult when the meter of a line or couplet is unknown. Scan each of the lines below and identify the meters. Note that the appearance of the lines can provide a clue to the meter, but it is not always a reliable guide, and the correct identification of vowel quantities is also required. The meters are as follows:

> iambic trimeter
> pure iambic trimeter
> iambic system
> first pythiambic
> second pythiambic
> choliambic
> galliambic

1. comes minore sum futurus in metu,
   qui maior absentes habet.

   Meter: _____

2. gaude sorte tua; me libertina, nec uno
   contenta, Phryne macerat.

   Meter: _____

3. hoc est quod unum est pro laboribus tantis;
   salue, o uenusta Sirmio, atque ero gaude.

   Meter: _____

4. quis hoc potest uidere, quis potest pati
   nisi impudicus et uorax et aleo?

   Meter: _____

5. roseis ut huic labellis sonitus citus abiit,
   geminas deorum ad aures noua nuntia referens . . .

   Meter: _____

6. uolente Circa membra, tunc mens et sonus
   relapsus atque notus in uultus honor.

   Meter: _____

7. uos, quibus est uirtus, muliebrem tollite luctum,
   Etrusca praeter et uolate litora.

   Meter: _____

EXERCISE LIII: JUMBLED IAMBICS

Unscramble the following iambic lines. 1–10 are trimeters, 11–15 are dimeters, and 16–20 are choliambics. There are no resolved feet, but elisions occur in lines 9, 10, 15, and 20.

1. remiges Vlixei laboriosi
2. uerberabit eques ungula sonante
3. caper libidinosus immolabitur
4. -que amputans falce inutiles ramos
5. lyra sonante carmen mixtum tibiis
6. cognosce, si iudicas; iube, si regnas
7. -que Titan diuidens clarum diem orbi
8. feror incerta uaecors non uaesana mente
9. nullum tempus ad nocendum est angustum malis
10. o sortem asperam et fata semper dura!
11. fortuna genus non mutat
12. ualent uenena Medeae
13. ilices trementes frangit
14. nauibus ustis fugit dux
15. Ilion obsessam accendit
16. est homo dicax et urbanus et uenustus
17. tam in se gaudet tamque ipse se miratur
18. quam libenter te inuiso quamque laetus
19. qui, cum librum malum legi, tunc me uocat
20. quare, Egnati bone, te mihi monendum est

EXERCISE LIV: IAMBIC STANZAS

Translate the following phrases and clauses into Latin iambics of the specified meters.

1. Trimeter

> Wintry Neptune beats with the deep salt-sea
> rocks (that are) no deafer to defenseless sailors.

> hibernus Neptunus altum salum tundo
> saxa non surdiora nudi nauitae

2. Iambic System

> They are silent and a white pallor tints their faces
>   and their stricken minds are dumbfounded

> taceo et albus pallor inficio ora
>   -que perculsae mentes stupeo

3. First Pythiambic

> as long as the wolf hostile to the flock and Orion hostile to sailors
>   should disturb the wintry sea

> dum lupus infestus pecus et Orion nautae
>   turbo hibernum mare

4. Second Pythiambic

> honey drips from the hollow ilex; from high mountains
>   the gentle water leaps down with splashing foot.

> mella mano ex caua ilex; alti montes
>   leuis lympha desilio crepans pes

5. Pure Trimeter

> he says he has stood on your summit
> and dipped his oars in your water.

> dico sto in tuum cacumen
> imbuo palmulae in tuum aequor.

6. Choliambics

> Therefore I, restored to health, give you greatest thanks
> because you (feminine) have not avenged my crime.

> quare refectus tu maximae grates
> ago, quod non ulciscor meum peccatum.

7. Galliambics

> A sluggish sleep covers their eyes with a tottering langor;
> in calm repose, the mind's raging fury departs.

> piger sopor operio hi (dat.) oculi labans langor;
> in mollis quies rabidus furor animus abeo.

EXERCISE LVA: IAMBICS FROM A PARAPHRASE

Translate the following witty lines about the city of Cologne into Latin choliambics. A paraphrase of the Rev. George Preston's solution is provided.

> In Köln, a town of monks and bones,
> And pavements fanged with murderous stones,
> And rags and hags and hideous wenches,
> I counted two and seventy stenches,
> All well defined, and several stinks.
> Ye nymphs, that reign o'er sewers and sinks,
> The river Rhine, it is well known,
> Doth wash your city of Cologne.
> But tell me, nymphs, what power divine
> Shall henceforth wash the river Rhine?

A city so abundant with bones, *monks*,[1] *rags*,[2]
Greeks, girls of filthy turpitude,
So (abundant with) the teeth of a paved *assassin*[3],
Cologne,[4] seventy-
Two *stenches*[5] – but each with its own odor –
(And) often *stinking*[6] noses I have noted in you.
O *nymphs*,[7] *trustees*[8] of *basins*[9] and *sewers*,[10]
The Rhine *washes*[11] that Colony, as is *well known*,[12]

---

[1] *popae* — the *popa* is properly "the priest's attendant, who killed the victim of a sacrifice" (*OLD*).
[2] *panni*
[3] *parricida*
[4] *Colonia Agrippina*
[5] *foetores*
[6] *putidi*
[7] *Nai*
[8] *praeses*
[9] *pelues*
[10] *cloacae*

But I pray, nymphs, tell me
What *divinity*[13] will have washed that *divine*[14] Rhine?

[11] place in the next line
[12] *satis notum*
[13] *numen*
[14] place in the previous line

EXERCISE LVB

Translate the following poem by Tennyson into Latin distichs of the "Iambic System" (trimeter and dimeter). A paraphrase adapted from Lupton's *Latin Lyric Verse Composition* is provided. According to Tennyson, the English poem was "made in a Lincolnshire lane at five o'clock in the morning, between blossoming hedges" in memory of Arthur Hallam.

> Break, break, break,
>> On thy cold gray stones, O Sea!
> And I would that my tongue could utter
>> The thoughts that arise in me.
>
> O, well for the fisherman's boy,
>> That he shouts with his sister at play!
> O, well for the sailor lad,
>> That he sings in his boat on the bay!
>
> And the stately ships go on
>> To their haven under the hill;
> But O for the touch of a vanish'd hand,
>> And the sound of a voice that is still!
>
> Break, break, break
>> At the foot of thy crags, O Sea!
> But the tender grace of a day that is dead
>> Will never come back to me.

Dash[1] your waters on the *rocks*,[2] surging sea,
Whose frigid shore is *cold*.[3]
My *obstructed*[4] voice refuses to speak the complaints
Rising in my mind.

---

[1] *illido*
[2] dative with *illido*
[3] *algeo*
[4] *impedita*

Happy (is)[5] the *seafaring*[6] boy, *whom*[7] it delights
To play with his sister
Or who, sitting in his hollow boat,
Free[8] from care renews his *song.*[9]

The ship *furrows*[10] the *salt-sea*[11] with proud impetus
Seeking[12] the *hollow*[13] of the harbor.
Who was to have *given*[14] me the voices and hands
Which oblivion buries?

Dash your waters on the rocks, surging sea,
Over which a rough *crag*[15] is *hanging.*[16]
Alas, how the sweet *grace*[17] of *past*[18] time
Refuses[19] to return to me.

---

[5] Think of Horace's second *Epode*: "Beatus ille. . . ."
[6] *nauticus*
[7] Place in the next line – a bold postponement but not inconsistent with Horatian practice.
[8] *solutus* + gen.
[9] *cantilena*
[10] *sulco*
[11] *salum*
[12] *appetens*
[13] *cauerna*
[14] *relinquo* (subjunctive)
[15] *cautes*
[16] *immineo*
[17] *decor*
[18] *actum*
[19] *denego*

Appendix: Metrical Tables

Feet

⌣ ⌣	pyrrhic
⌣ −	iamb
− ⌣	trochee
− −	spondee
⌣ ⌣ ⌣	tribrach
⌣ ⌣ −	anapest
⌣ − ⌣	amphibrach
− ⌣ ⌣	dactyl
− ⌣ −	cretic
⌣ − −	bacchius
− − −	molossus
⌣ ⌣ ⌣ ⌣	proceleusmatic
− ⌣ ⌣ −	choriamb
⌣ − − ⌣	antispastus
− − ⌣ ⌣	major ionic
⌣ ⌣ − −	minor ionic
− ⌣ ⌣ ⌣	first paeon
⌣ − ⌣ ⌣	second paeon
⌣ ⌣ − ⌣	third paeon
⌣ ⌣ ⌣ −	fourth paeon
⌣ − − −	first epitrite
− ⌣ − −	second epitrite
− − ⌣ −	third epitrite
− − − ⌣	fourth epitrite
⌣ − ⌣ −	diiamb
− ⌣ − ⌣	ditrochee
− − − −	dispondee

Lines

The basic rhythmic patterns for 26 common lines are given below. Note that further variations may be possible but depend on the specific practices of individual poets. Many of these lines are discussed in greater depth in the body of the text.

dactylic hexameter	$- \smile\smile \mid - \smile\smile \mid - \parallel \smile\smile \mid - \smile\smile \mid - \smile\smile \mid - \bar{\smile}$
dactylic pentameter	$- \smile\smile \mid - \smile\smile \mid - \parallel - \smile\smile \mid - \smile\smile \mid \bar{\smile}$
dactylic tetrameter	$- \smile\smile \mid - \smile\smile \mid - \smile\smile \mid - \bar{\smile}^{1}$
dactylic trimeter catalectic[2]	$- \smile\smile \mid - \smile\smile \mid \bar{\smile}$
Adonic	$- \smile\smile \mid - \bar{\smile}$
anapestic dimeter	$\smile\smile - \mid \smile\smile - \mid \smile\smile - \smile\smile$ or
	$- \smile\smile \mid \smile\smile - \mid - \smile\smile \mid \smile\smile -^{3}$
anapestic monometer	$\smile\smile - \mid \smile\smile -$
hendecasyllable	$- - - \smile\smile - \smile - \smile - \bar{\smile}$ or
	$- \smile - \smile\smile - \smile - \smile - \bar{\smile}$ or
	$\smile - - \smile\smile - \smile - \smile - \bar{\smile}$
Sapphic[4]	$- \smile - - - \parallel \smile\smile - \smile - \bar{\smile}$
greater Sapphic	$- \smile - - - \smile\smile - \parallel - \smile\smile - \smile - \bar{\smile}$
Alcaic[5]	$\bar{\smile} - \smile - - \parallel - \smile\smile - \smile \bar{\smile}$
Alcaic enneasyllabic[6]	$\bar{\smile} - \smile - - - \smile - \bar{\smile}$
Alcaic decasyllabic	$- \smile\smile - \smile\smile - \smile - \bar{\smile}$
lesser Asclepiad	$- - - \smile\smile - \parallel - \smile\smile - \smile \bar{\smile}$
greater Asclepiad	$- - - \smile\smile - \parallel - \smile\smile - \parallel - \smile\smile - \smile \bar{\smile}$
Glyconic	$- \bar{\smile} - \smile\smile - \smile \bar{\smile}$
Pherecratean	$- \bar{\smile} - \smile\smile - \bar{\smile}$
iambic dimeter	$\bar{\smile} - \mid \smile \smile\smile \mid \bar{\smile} - \mid \smile \bar{\smile}$
iambic trimeter	$\smile - \mid \smile - \mid \smile - \mid \smile - \mid \smile - \mid \smile \bar{\smile}^{7}$

[1] Seneca sometimes uses a dactyl or a cretic in the last foot.

[2] Lines in which the term "catalectic" appears occur most commonly (or only) in the catalectic form, but other lines can also be made catalectic by "stopping short" or taking away the final syllable. The dactylic trimeter catalectic is the same as the second hemistich of a pentameter.

[3] A dactyl may take the place of an anapest or spondee in the first and third feet.

[4] The line is also known as the "lesser Sapphic" or the "Sapphic hendecasyllable."

[5] The line is also known as the "Alcaic hendecasyllable."

[6] The line is a variation of trochaic dimeter (see below).

[7] Spondees and anapests can be used in the odd numbered feet, and dactyls can be used in feet one and three. In addition, the long syllables are occasionally resolved into two shorts. A "pure iambic trimeter" consists of six iambs with no substitutions allowed.

choliambic (= scazon)[8]	∪ − | ∪ − | ∪ − | ∪ − | ∪ − | ∪ ⏒
galliambic	∪ ∪ − ∪ − ∪ − − ‖ ∪ ∪ − ∪ ∪ ∪ ⏒
ithyphallic	− ∪ | − ∪ | − ⏒
greater Archilochian	− ⏖ | − ⏖ | − ‖ ⏖ | − ⏖ | − ∪ | − ∪ | − ⏒
Aristophanic	− ∪ ∪ | − ∪ | − ⏒
trochaic tetrameter catalectic	− ∪ | − ⏒ | − ∪ | − ⏒ ‖ − ∪ | − ⏒ | − ∪ | ⏒[9]
trochaic dimeter catalectic[10]	− ∪ | − ∪ | − ∪ | ⏒

---

[8] Also known as a limping iambic, the line is like an iambic trimeter but must have an iamb in the fifth foot and a trochee or spondee in the sixth. In addition, the natural word accent typically falls on the penultimate syllable of the line.

[9] The long syllables are occasionally resolved into two shorts.

[10] The line is also known as a "Euripidean" verse.

Meters

Stichic Meters (singles lines of the same type)

      dactylic hexameter
      dactylic tetrameter
      anapestic dimeter
      first Asclepiad (= "lesser Asclepiad")
      fifth Asclepiad (= "greater Asclepiad")
      hendecasyllabic
      iambic trimeter
      choliambic
      galliambic
      trochaic tetrameter catalectic

Distichs (two lines of different types)

      Elegiac couplet (= dactylic hexameter and pentameter)
$$-\,\overline{\cup\cup}\,\mid\,-\,\overline{\cup\cup}\,\mid\,-\,\|\,\overline{\cup\cup}\mid\,-\,\overline{\cup\cup}\,\mid\,-\,\underline{\cup\cup}\mid\,-\,\overline{\cup}$$
$$-\,\overline{\cup\cup}\,\mid\,-\,\overline{\cup\cup}\,\mid\,-\,\|\,-\,\,\underline{\cup\cup}\mid\,\overline{\cup}$$

      Alcmanian (= dactylic hexameter and tetrameter)
$$-\,\overline{\cup\cup}\mid\,-\,\overline{\cup\cup}\mid\,-\,\|\,\overline{\cup\cup}\mid\,-\,\overline{\cup\cup}\mid\,-\,\underline{\cup\cup}\mid\,-\,\overline{\cup}$$
$$-\,\overline{\cup\cup}\mid\,-\,\overline{\cup\cup}\mid\,-\,\|\,-\,\underline{\cup\cup}\mid\,\overline{\cup}$$

      Third Asclepiad (= glyconic and lesser asclepiad)
$$-\,\overline{\cup}\,-\,\cup\,\cup\,-\,\cup\,\overline{\cup}$$
$$-\,-\,-\,\cup\,\cup\,-\,\|\,-\,\cup\,\cup\,-\,\cup\,\overline{\cup}$$

      Iambic distich (= iambic trimeter[11] and dimeter)
$$\cup\,-\,\mid\,\cup\,-\,\mid\,\cup\,-\,\mid\,\cup\,-\,\mid\,\cup\,-\,\mid\,\cup\,\overline{\cup}$$
$$\overline{\cup}\,-\,\mid\,\cup\,\overline{\cup\cup}\,\mid\,\overline{\cup}\,-\,\mid\,\cup\,\overline{\cup}$$

      First Archilochian (= dactylic hexameter and dactylic trimeter catalectic)
$$-\,\overline{\cup\cup}\mid\,-\,\overline{\cup\cup}\mid\,-\,\|\,\overline{\cup\cup}\mid\,-\,\overline{\cup\cup}\mid\,-\,\underline{\cup\cup}\mid\,-\,\overline{\cup}$$
$$-\,\underline{\cup\cup}\mid\,-\,\underline{\cup\cup}\mid\,\overline{\cup}$$

---

[11] See Table of Lines for a full account of possible substitutions in the iambic trimeter.

Second Archilochian (= dactylic hexameter and iambic dimeter + dactylic
  trimeter catalectic)

$$- \overline{\cup\cup} \mid - \overline{\cup\cup} \mid - \parallel \overline{\cup\cup} \mid - \overline{\cup\cup} \mid - \overline{\cup\cup} \mid - \overline{\cup}$$
$$\overline{\cup} - \mid \cup \overline{\cup\cup} \mid \overline{\cup} - \mid \cup \overline{\cup} \parallel - \overline{\cup\cup} \mid - \overline{\cup\cup} \mid \overline{\cup}$$

Third Archilochian (iambic trimeter and iambic dimeter + dactylic trimeter
  catalectic)

$$\cup - \mid \cup - \mid \cup - \mid \cup - \mid \cup - \mid \cup \overline{\cup}$$
$$\overline{\cup} - \mid \cup \overline{\cup\cup} \mid \overline{\cup} - \mid \cup \overline{\cup} \parallel - \overline{\cup\cup} \mid - \overline{\cup\cup} \mid \overline{\cup}$$

Fourth Archilochian (= greater Archilochian and iambic trimeter catalectic)

$$- \overline{\cup\cup} \mid - \overline{\cup\cup} \mid - \parallel \overline{\cup\cup} \mid - \overline{\cup\cup} \mid - \cup \mid - \cup \mid - \overline{\cup}$$
$$\cup - \mid \cup - \mid \cup - \mid \cup - \mid \cup - \mid \overline{\cup}$$

Hipponactean (trochaic dimeter catalectic and iambic trimeter catalectic)

$$- \cup \mid - \cup \mid - \cup \mid \overline{\cup}$$
$$\cup \overline{\cup\cup} \mid \cup \overline{\cup\cup} \mid \cup \overline{\cup\cup} \mid \cup \overline{\cup\cup} \mid \overline{\cup} - \mid \overline{\cup}$$

Greater Sapphic Distich (Aristophanic and Greater Sapphic)

$$- \cup \cup \mid - \cup \mid - \overline{\cup}$$
$$- \cup - - - \cup \cup - \parallel - \cup \cup - \cup - \overline{\cup}$$

Stanzas (groups of four mixed lines)

Sapphic Stanza

$$- \cup - - - \parallel \cup \cup - \cup - \overline{\cup}$$
$$- \cup - - - \parallel \cup \cup - \cup - \overline{\cup}$$
$$- \cup - - - \parallel \cup \cup - \cup - \overline{\cup}$$
$$- \overline{\cup\cup} \mid - \overline{\cup}$$

Alcaic Stanza

$$\overline{\cup} - \cup - - \parallel - \cup \cup - \cup \overline{\cup}$$
$$\overline{\cup} - \cup - - \parallel - \cup \cup - \cup \overline{\cup}$$
$$\overline{\cup} - \cup - - - \cup - \overline{\cup}$$
$$- \cup \cup - \cup \cup - \cup - \overline{\cup}$$

Second Asclepiad

— — — ∪ ∪ — ‖ — ∪ ∪ — ∪ ×
— — — ∪ ∪ — ‖ — ∪ ∪ — ∪ ×
— — — ∪ ∪ — ‖ — ∪ ∪ — ∪ ×
— × — ∪ ∪ — ∪ ×

Third Asclepiad

— — — ∪ ∪ — ‖ — ∪ ∪ — ∪ ×
— — — ∪ ∪ — ‖ — ∪ ∪ — ∪ ×
— × — ∪ ∪ — ×
— × — ∪ ∪ — ∪ ×

GLOSSARY OF TERMS

acephalic   Lit. "without a head." An acephalic line lacks the ini-
                         tial syllable of the expected rhythm.

alliteration   The repetition of the same sound beginning several
                         words in sequence; called "*paromoeon*" by the Greeks
                         and Romans.

anacrusis   Lit. "striking up." An initial syllable, or "upbeat," be-
                         fore the normal rhythm of a line commences.

anaphora   The repetition of a word or phrase at the beginning of
                         successive phrases, clauses, or lines.

antithesis   A rhetorical contrast or opposition of ideas. Antithesis
                         juxtaposes words and phrases with opposing mean-
                         ings, usually in parallel syntax (sentence structure).

aposiopesis   Greek for "becoming silent." A rhetorical device in
                         which the speaker stops in mid-sentence. [A clue from
                         the (London) Sunday Times crossword puzzle asked:
                         "To be or not to . . . ." 11 letters. The solution:
                         aposiopesis.]

apostrophe   A rhetorical device in which a speaker addresses some-
                         one (or something, an abstraction for example) who is
                         not present.

arsis   Properly the unaccented second half of a metrical foot
                         (i.e. the two short syllables of a dactyl, the single short
                         syllable of the trochee, or the second long syllable of
                         the spondee). Arsis is literally the "rise" of the metri-
                         cal foot that corresponds with the rise of the bodily
                         foot in the dances that accompanied the performance
                         of much Greek poetry. *Thesis is the down-beat
                         or "fall" of the foot. Note, however, that Roman

201

grammarians, who studied poetry apart from dance, thought of arsis as the rise of the *voice* at the *start* of a foot, effectively reversing the terms. This backwards usage persists in the works of some modern writers, so be careful. It is a shame that there has to be so much fuss over a term that contributes little of significance to the understanding and appreciation of poetry.

asyndeton The lack of conjunctions between coordinate phrases, clauses, or words.

caesura 1) a slight rhythmic pause in a line of verse that occurs at prescribed intervals, and 2) a break between words within a metrical foot. Derived from the verb *caedere*, the caesura literally "cuts" or divides the line.

catachresis The misuse of a word; the illogical and inappropriate extension of a word's meaning.

catalectic Lacking the final (usually short) syllable expected in a line of verse; a hexameter with a trochaic ending ($-\cup$) may be called "catalectic" because it lacks the final short syllable of the dactyl ($-\cup\cup$).

chiasmus In rhetoric, chiasmus is the reversal of grammatical structures in successive phrases or clauses. Derived from the Greek letter chi (χ), chiasmus can refer any criss-crossing of linguistic elements.

conceit A figure of speech that establishes an elaborate and striking parallel between two dissimilar things.

correption The shortening of a long vowel or diphthong that precedes another vowel; sometimes called "epic correption" because it occurs in Homer and was imitated by subsequent writers in the epic tradition.

diaeresis Literally "division" – 1) a division between words corresponding to the end of a metrical foot; 2) the division of two consecutive vowels into separate

syllables or the transformation of a consonantal *u* or
i into a vowel.

didactic poetry Poetry that teaches either moral or practical lessons,
e.g., Vergil's *Georgics.*

dithyramb A poem honoring the god Dionysius. Dithyrambs were
sung and accompanied by dancing.

elegy Often etymologized as "to say 'alas! alas!,'" the term
elegy generally refers to a poem of lamentation. *Love
elegy*, a type of poem written by Ovid and others,
specifically laments the trials and tribulations of (typically unrequited) love, often in a humorous way. In its
strict, classical usage, however, the term elegy refers
to the *meter* of the poem (the elegiac couplet – a
dactylic hexameter followed by a pentameter), not its
subject matter. Accordingly, not all ancient elegies are
about lamentation.

elision The suppression or "striking out" of a final vowel or
diphthong (or a final *m* with its preceding vowel) by a
vowel (or an *h* plus a vowel) at the start of the next word.

epic A long narrative poem in the grand style, usually
with a "long line" (e.g., the *dactylic hexameter* in
classical Greek and Latin epic or the *iambic pentameter* in English epics like Milton's *Paradise Lost*).
As the Roman critic Horace wrote, following
Callimachus, epics are usually about "kings and battles" and typically involve the destiny of a people —
their history, traditions, and values.

epithet An (often compound) adjective that is used repeat-
edly to describe a person or object, e.g., "the wine-
dark sea" or "swift-footed Achilles" in Homer.

figure [Or "figure of speech"] Any use of language that
departs from the usual, standard, literal meaning of
words in order to suggest some other meaning or

effect. Ancient rhetorical theory differentiated loosely between "tropes" (see entry below), which extend the meanings of words in a variety of special ways, and "schemes," which achieve their effect by the way in which the words are arranged. Examples in this glossary include: antithesis, aposiopesis, apostrophe, catachresis, chiasmus, irony, metaphor, metonymy, prosopopoeia, simile, and synecdoche.

foot The combination of two, three, or four syllables that recur in a line of poetry. See the Table of Metrical Feet that precedes this glossary.

genre A type or category of writing. Literary genres rely upon an established and widely (although seldom universally) accepted set of rules and conventions that serve to differentiate one kind of literature from another. Generic classification is based chiefly on the formal structure of a work and/or its subject matter, but may also take into account such things as length, function, style, or other factors. Aristotle divided poetry into three large genres: lyric, epic (or narrative), and drama.

hephthemimeral caesura A caesura that occurs after the first long syllable of the fourth foot, i.e. after seven (hept-) half-feet.

hiatus A slight break or "gap" between vowels that prevents an expected elision from taking place. Hiatus typically occurs at the caesura and corresponds with a sense break.

hypermetric Having an extra (usually short) syllable in a line of verse. To resolve this irregularity, the hypermetric syllable is typically elided by a vowel at the start of the next line. The term "hypercatalectic" is sometimes used as a synonym.

irony In rhetoric, irony is the use of a word in a manner that conveys a meaning opposite to the word's literal meaning. In a broader sense, irony is the (sometimes humorous) inconsistency that occurs when a seemingly straightforward statement or event is undermined by the context in which it occurs so as to give it a different, opposite significance. The term was first used in literary criticism to describe a stock character in Greek comedy — the *eiron* (or "dissembler") who feigned ignorance and stupidity but in the end was always victorious over the self-confident, but genuinely stupid, braggart.

metaphor   An implied comparison between two distinct things that are basically unlike but nonetheless share something in common. Whereas a *simile* states the comparison using the words "like" or "as" (Achilles *is like* a lion), metaphor does not (Achilles *is* a lion). But not all metaphors look like similes with the words "like" and "as" removed; comparison may be implied in other ways. Some metaphors will tell you *the manner in which* A is similar to B without explicitly telling you what B is: "on the final examination, several students went down in flames." This is a metaphor. Students who have not studied adequately for their exams cannot literally "go down in flames" but are similar to crashing war planes shot from the sky inasmuch as they both suffer devastating failure and defeat.

meter   The abstract but regular rhythmic pattern that governs a line of verse; from *metiri*, "to measure." In antiquity, meter was widely regarded as a crucial component of poetry and was often dictated by a poem's genre.

metonymy   The substitution of some attribute of a person, object, or abstraction for that person, object, or abstraction itself, e.g., crown for royalty, brass for military officers, White House for the President and/or his staff, Vergil for the writings of Dante, etc. Metonymy, which literally means "change of name," always replaces the name of one thing with the name of another that is closely associated with it.

ode　　　　　　　　　From the Greek for "song," an ode is a lyric poem on a serious and (usually) lofty subject. The ode has an elaborate formal structure and uses grand or elevated language. The ode derives from the choral songs of Greek tragedy, and Pindar was one of the most prominent poets to develop its form. The Roman poet Horace also wrote odes.

onomatopoeia　　　　The use of words that in some way imitate the sound they refer to (e.g., hiss, buzz, etc.). Vergil often wrote entire lines whose rhythm duplicates their subject matter (e.g., *quadripedante putrem sonitu quatit ungula campum* – "with a four-footed sound, the hoof smashes against the dusty plain").

oxymoron　　　　　　The combination of two contradictory terms: "living death," "darkness visible" (Milton), etc.

paean　　　　　　　　A hymn to the god Apollo; any song of rejoicing; a victory song (military or otherwise).

paradox　　　　　　　A seemingly self-contradictory statement that actually turns out to make sense on some other level. Paradox is often used to question "normal" or accepted modes of thought and understanding, as in Shakespeare's "the truest poetry is the most feigning."

paratactic　　　　　　Literally "side by side arrangement." The adjective paratactic refers to a sequence of clauses or sentences placed one after another without any indication of their connection or relationship. A paratactic style is marked by the absence of all coordinating and subordinating conjunctions other than "and." As such, causal and temporal relationships between sentences is often unclear. The term paratactic may be applied on a larger narrative scale as well and denotes a lack of specified relationships among various stories or events. The opposite of paratactic is hypotactic.

parody	An exaggerated and mocking imitation of the form, style, and/or subject matter of another literary work (or author or genre). Parody typically involves either the serious treatment of a ridiculous subject or (less frequently) the ridiculous treatment of a serious subject.
pastoral	A poem about country life in which a shepherd (*pastor*) is usually the speaker. Some pastoral poems, or "eclogues," take the form of a dialogue or singing contest between two shepherds.
penthemimeral caesura	A caesura that occurs after the first long syllable of the third foot, i.e. after five (pent-) half-feet.
persona	The assumed, fictional identity (the Latin word *persona* means "mask," something that the voice "sounds through") of the speaker of a lyric poem or narrator of a story. The persona is a fictional construct not to be confused with the author, although sometimes the pretense of the persona as "true voice" of the author is maintained.
prodelision	Elision of the first syllable of a word (usually *est*) by the final syllable of the previous word. See "elision."
prosopopoeia	The Greek term for personification; lit. "making a face" (for something that doesn't ordinarily have one). Personifications may occur in passing or be developed as actual characters.
rhythm	The sequence of long and short or accented and unaccented syllables in a line of verse. Whereas *meter pertains to the abstract pattern governing the entire poem, rhythm refers to the specific cadence of any given line; thus prose can have rhythm but not meter.
satire	A genre that derides, or makes fun of, the failings of individuals and/or society, sometimes with the corrective aim of closing the gap between real and ideal

situations. Satires range in tone from amusement to contempt and often include passages of vulgar humor.

scansion The practice of determining and marking the long and short syllables in a poem.

simile A simile is an explicit comparison between two distinct things and always uses the words "like" or "as." An *epic* simile is an extended, detailed, and highly stylized simile whose lengthy description appears to digress from but in some way expands upon the main narrative action of the poem.

synaphea The term "synaphea" is used when two lines "share" a single metrical structure such that the principles of elision, hiatus, and lengthening by position extend across the line division to create, in effect, a single continuous line.

synecdoche Greek for "taking together." A synecdoche is a figure of speech in which a part stands for the whole (e.g. *hands* for *workmen, sail* for *ship*, etc.) or species stands for genus (e.g. *bread* for *food*). The whole may also be used to signify a part, but this is less common.

synizesis Literally the "stitching together" or joining into a single syllable of two consecutive vowels that do not ordinarily form a diphthong.

theme A general concept or idea articulated (usually indirectly) by a literary work. Themes are abstractions that are distinct from yet derivative of a work's subject matter (i.e. the people, objects, situations, events, etc. it describes).

thesis Thesis is literally the "placing" (of the foot), i.e. the accented first syllable of the metrical foot that corresponds with the fall of the dancing foot. See "arsis."

threnos Greek term for a dirge or funeral lament (sometimes called a threnody). One of the oldest types of lyric poetry.

topos
Greek for "place." A *topos* is a conspicuous and definable "commonplace" or "topic," an incident, situation, device, or formula that occurs frequently in literature. Sometimes called a "motif."

trope
A "turn of phrase" (from the Greek verb meaning "to turn"); a figure of speech (see "figure" above). In classical rhetoric, tropes are used to twist words away from their usual, literal meanings in order to suggest some other meaning and to have a persuasive effect on the listener (or reader).

verisimilitude
The semblance or illusion of reality in literature. This implies excluding things that are improbable or disguising the improbable so as to make it *seem* real.

MODERN LATIN POETS REPRESENTED IN THE EXERCISES

The composition of Latin verse was such a vital part of a classical education in the 1800s that dozens of exercise books and thousands of Latin poems were published during the nineteenth century alone. While many of the exercises in this volume are based on the ancient poets themselves, exercises that require the translation of English poetry into Latin are necessarily based upon the work of modern writers. Brief biographical sketches of some of these "contributors" are given here. It should be recognized that fine Latin verse comes not only from such noted classicists as Charles Anthon, Benjamin Hall Kennedy, Sir Richard Claverhouse Jebb, and John Percival Postgate, but also from lesser-know figures like William Baker and George Preston, whose work is perhaps even more accomplished than that of their more famous colleagues.

Charles Anthon (1797–1867) was Professor of Classics and the Jay Professor of the Greek Language and Literature in Columbia College. He was the author of Greek and Latin grammar books, a classical dictionary, a well-known edition of Caesar's *Gallic War*, and several volumes pertaining to the composition of Greek and Latin prose and verse. Of particular note is his *System of Latin Versification*, which remains a valuable resource for the modern student.

The Rev. William Baker, D.D. (1841–1910) was Headmaster of the Merchant Taylors' School and formerly Fellow and Tutor of St. John's College, Oxford. Although Baker is not known to posterity as a classicist of particular distinction, his *Greek and Latin Versions* is a highly polished collection of 100 translations of English poetry into Greek and Latin verse. Many exercises in the text in hand are based upon Baker's "solutions" to Oxford verse composition scholarship examinations.

Robinson Ellis (1834–1913), who is perhaps best known as a teacher of paleography, was Honorary Fellow of Trinity College, Oxford, and the Corpus Professor of Latin. A champion of verse composition in the schools and colleges, Ellis also experimented with classical meters in English poetry. He was a frequent contributor to Victorian collections of Latin verse.

Gerard Manley Hopkins (1844–1889) studied under Benjamin Jowett at Bailiol College, Oxford, was ordained as a Jesuit priest in 1877, and became chairman of Greek at Dublin in 1884. Although best known for his English poems, Hopkins also wrote in Greek, Latin, and Welsh.

Sir Richard Claverhouse Jebb (1841–1905) was one of the founders of the Cambridge Philological Society and is perhaps best known as a commentator, translator, and textual critic of Sophocles. His translation of Browning's "Abt Vogler" into Pindaric Greek is said to have surpassed the original, and he was also the author of *Translations into Greek and Latin Verse*.

The Rev. Benjamin Hall Kennedy, D.D. (1804–1889), in whose name the prestigious "Kennedy Professor of Latin" chair was established at Cambridge, was Headmaster at Shrewsbury and a Reader in Classics at St John's. He was the author of a *Public School Latin Grammar*, a *Latin Primer*, and a substantial body of Latin poetry, some of which appeared in his *Between Whiles*. Along with colleague Montagu Butler, for whom the Butler Prize in Latin Verse Composition is named, Kennedy is reputed to have had "habitual recourse to verse composition in every quiet hour." An authority on Greek drama, Kennedy also wrote a textbook on Greek verse composition.

Joseph Hirst Lupton (1836–1905) was Surmaster of St. Paul's School and the author of two textbooks: *An Introduction to Latin Elegiac Verse Composition* and *An Introduction to Latin Lyric Verse Composition*. Several of Lupton's exercises have served as models for exercises in the present volume. A man of wide-ranging interests and abilities, Lupton also published an edition of More's *Utopia*, several theological works, and the *Life of John Colet*, Dean of St. Paul's.

John Percival Postgate (1853–1926), Fellow and sometime Senior Lecturer of Trinity College, Cambridge, supplied editions of Catullus, Tibullus, Propertius, and Lucan that were for many years the texts of choice. His *Prosodia Latina* (although now often relegated to obscure storage places in college libraries) remains a useful manual. Some of his own Greek and Latin verse may be found in his *Translation and Translations*.

The Rev. George Preston (1840–1913) was Fellow of Magdalene College, Cambridge, and author of *Exercises in Latin Verse*. Although there is practically no biographical information available about him, Preston produced many verses that are remarkable models of clarity, Latinity, and metrical refinement.

Robert Yelverton Tyrrell (1844–1914) was Fellow of Trinity College, Oxford, and formerly Professor of Greek at Dublin, where he edited the *Dublin Translations*, a large collection of Greek and Latin verse by various hands. Tyrrell also produced editions of Cicero's letters and the *Miles Gloriosus* of Plautus.

BIBLIOGRAPHY

Anthon, Charles. *A System of Latin Versification*. New York: Harper & Brothers, 1845.

Bradley, Charles. *Exercises in Latin Prosody and Versification*, 3rd edition. London: A.J. Valpy, 1820.

Burnet, Richard. *Various English and Latin Poems*. Norwich: R.M. Bacon, 1808.

Crusius, Friedrich. *Römische Metrik*. Munich: Max Hueber, 1955.

Fordyce, C.J. *Catullus: A Commentary*. Oxford: OUP, 1961.

Heinze, R. *Die lyrischen Verse des Horaz*. Leipzig, 1959.

Kenney, E.J. *Ovid: Heroides 16–21*. Cambridge: CUP, 1996.

Lateiner, D. "Mimetic Syntax: Metaphor from Word Order, Especially in Ovid," *AJPh* 111 (1990): 204–37.

Lupton, J.H. *An Introduction to Latin Elegiac Verse Composition*. London: Macmillan, 1898.

Lupton, J.H. *An Introduction to Latin Lyric Verse Composition*. London: Macmillan, 1927.

Marouzeau, J. *L'ordre des mots en latin*. Paris, 1953.

McKeown, J.C. *Ovid: Amores*. Liverpool: Francis Cairns, 1987.

Nisbet, R.G.M. and M. Hubbard. *A Commentary on Horace, Odes, Book 1*. Oxford: Clarendon Press, 1970.

———. *A Commentary on Horace, Odes, Book 2*. Oxford: Clarendon Press, 1978.

Papillon, T.L. and A.E. Haigh. *Virgil*. Oxford: Clarendon Press, 1892.

Pinsky, Robert. *The Sounds of Poetry: A Brief Guide*. New York: Farrar, Straus and Giroux, 1998.

Platnauer, Maurice. *Latin Elegiac Verse*. Cambridge: CUP, 1951.

Postgate, J.P. *Prosodia Latina*. Oxford: Clarendon Press, 1923.

Preston, George. *Exercises in Latin Verse*. London: Macmillan, 1889.

Richardson, L.J. "Horace's Alcaic Strophe," *Classical Philology* 1, 6 (1907): 175–204.

Skutsch, O. *The Annals of Q. Ennius*. Oxford: Clarendon Press, 1985.

Thomas, R.F. *Virgil: Georgics*. Cambridge: CUP, 1988.

West, M.L. *Greek Metre*. Oxford: Clarendon Press, 1982.

Whitfield, B.G. *A Classical Handbook for Sixth Forms*, Oxford: Blackwell, 1956.

Wilkinson, L.P. *Golden Latin Artistry*. Cambridge: CUP, 1963.

———. *Horace and His Lyric Poetry*. Cambridge: CUP, 1946.

Williams, R.D. *Virgil: The Eclogues and Georgics*. New York: St. Martin's Press, 1979.

Winbolt, S.E. *Latin Hexameter Verse*. London: Methuen, 1903.

Young, A.M. "The Pictoral Arrangement of Words in Vergil," *TAPA* 64 (1933).